2:12 a.m.

Essays

2:12 a.m.
Essays

Kat Meads

Stephen F. Austin State University Press
Nacogdoches ★ Texas

Stephen F. Austin State University Press
PO Box 13007, SFA Station
Nacogdoches, TX 75962
sfapress@sfasu.edu
936-468-1078

For information about special discounts for bulk purchases, please contact Texas A&M University Press Consortium sharon-mills@tamu.edu or 800.826.8911

Book Design: Laura Davis
Cover Art: Philip Rosenthal

Printed in the United States of America

LIBRARY OF CONGRESS IN PUBLICATION DATA
Meads, Kat
2:12 a.m.: essays / Kat Meads. — 1st ed.
p. cm.
ISBN: 978-1-62288-039-3

I. Meads, Kat.

CONTENTS

In Preface

Night and Its Houndings

Tell a dream, lose a reader, warned Henry James, but to get to dream(s) interrupted, where else to start?

I was living, sleeping, on the second floor of a house close enough to the Pacific Ocean to hear the grunts of sea lions in the early hours before traffic competed. From twilight to dawn, a street lamp shone through my bedroom window, half lighting, half concealing the furniture, the walls, the carpet, the sheets. My bed faced the doorway. Positioned between me and that exit the night I started awake—or thought I started awake—a shadowy someone, standing to the left of the mirror, offside the dresser. A very still, very passive presence, that someone. Slightly built, shoulders slumped, hair mussed, clothes loose, young or youngish in age. Stared at, he didn't move or speak. Aside from the speed-freak pounding of my heart, I didn't move or speak. But even under the influence of accelerating panic, I thought the stranger in my room came across less menacing than aggrieved.

A stranger, nonetheless.

In my bedroom.

Post-midnight.

I remember, in the dream, working hard to convince myself that I was indeed dreaming and blinked to make the uninvited disappear. It was only after the blinking experiment failed, my visitor holding steady, that I screamed and threw myself out of bed with intentions of escape.

It was the screaming that woke me for real—at 2:12 a.m.

Hints, portents: that night, that hour, that dream messenger come like an archangel of the goddess Nyx to warn of rough and rougher nights ahead, screams no solution to the plight of wakefulness and what wakefulness exaggerated: flashing headlights, the bounce and rattle of beer cans, the act of coition as prepared for and performed in the apartment across the way, the clacking toenails of a Rhodesian Ridgeback in his night pen next door.

A revolt of the body and the mind is insomnia.

The first, faint ringing of the mortality bell is insomnia.

An unwelcome replay of regrets and recriminations, a red-eye tour of the world at large and the world within is insomnia.

Night at its stalker best.

Mr. James turns up again in these pages as does evidence of a persistent fascination with a country not my own. My father appears often, in life, in death, in and among the relatives and citizens of a North Carolina crossroads community I left many, many years ago but a place that will not leave me.

A baby boomer, a child of the Cold War, a Sixties romantic, a middle-age fatalist with the desires, fixations, confusions and disappointments those categories suggest.

All intricately part of my night script.

All grist for the insomnia mill.

In the South

The Making of an Insomniac

Once upon a time, in paradise since lost, lived a sleep-indulged, sleep-happy girl who fell asleep whenever, wherever and stayed asleep at length and at will.

A deep-dreaming sleep junkie she was, very much her father's child.

After six days of hard field labor, this father, Dubby, devoted his after-church Sunday afternoons to napping on the living room couch. Certainly he deserved the rest. Added to the constant worry of equipment breakdowns and field pests: the grueling effort of digging drains with a shovel and weeding soybeans with a hoe. During planting and harvest seasons, he worked first to final light and he worked solo, unable to afford the expense of hired help.

On those Sunday afternoons while Dubby napped, his daughter stared. Not for purposes of mischief or mayhem. It soothed the daughter to watch her father sleep. Sometimes she'd bring in a cat or dog to watch along with her. Occasionally she'd ape the deep breathing, chest swell for chest swell, fake snore for real snore. When her father opened an eye and caught her hovering, never did he ask what she was up to or shoo her elsewhere. He'd grunt, say "hey," roll over on his side and drift off again, the very image of peace.

Or so I recall.

But who can trust memory any more than fairy tales?

When I was ten, a neighbor ran over the family cur and crushed his right hip, dog bones no match for a Chevy truck. From necessity and through experience, farmers tend to be unsentimental, fatalistic folk. My parents' generation expected to lose dogs, cats, pigs, cows and horses the same way they expected hurricanes to blow in periodically from the Atlantic and devastate in a few hours what had taken six months to grow. Kids are more stubborn in their fate-resisting, also more melodramatic. Clinging to my wounded dog, I bawled and begged until my father broke precedent and agreed to a vet visit.

A poor farmer, yes, but also a daddy.

Dr. Dahl of Elizabeth City worked out of an office attached to his house and wore khaki, uniform fashion, shirt and trousers. Besides the implements of his trade, his office contained stacks of pulp fiction, pride of place going to James M. Cain. A taste for sensationalist fiction, a livelihood earned by patching up the bloody and broken—there's laudable symmetry in that pairing. While my father and I waited, Dr. Dahl patched up our broken critter and afterward sent the three of us on our way with a grocery bag full of suggested reading.

While recuperating, the dog snoozed on the back porch. During that period, my father also napped on the back porch, the ailing dog resting his paw on Dubby's shoulder as if the two were longtime sleeping buds. My mother noticed the shift from couch to porch and commented on it; I also noticed and reoriented my sleep watch, gazing through the screen at the two of them from a kitchen chair. Anyone trying to get in or out of the house while they snoozed had to use the front door, the back entrance blocked by dreamers. My mother complained because their obstacle threw off her ramped up/waste-no-motion timing, but I didn't mind the detour, perfectly willing to circle the house or slog a mile of ditches if need be.

My daddy and my dog were sleeping. I couldn't have wished better for either.

During our pre-teen years, on Friday nights, my best friend, Shirley, often slept over at my house. We'd gab until we conked out—typically toward dawn—then make up the deficit by sleeping till noon, unaware and undisturbed by the hustle and bang of breakfast prep, morning chores, the perpetual slamming of screen doors. Around midday we'd rise, primp, chow down on cheeseburgers, bat a tennis ball back and forth, adjourn inside and resume our marathon chat, prelude to another conk out.

Sheer bliss, the entire schedule.

Those of us who ventured off to sleep-away camp in Currituck County during the 1960s boarded a borrowed church bus and made the trip to the 4-H camp in Manteo. The Head/Heart/Hands/Health enterprise, added to the U.S. Department of Agriculture's Cooperative Extension Program in 1914, championed the learn-by-doing approach and rewarded industrious farmers' kids with ribbons blue, white and red. During the school year, we 4-H-ers completed and wrote up individual projects (how to cook deviled eggs, how to raise brood sows) and come the summer gathered en masse along the shores of the Croatan Sound. Concrete defined our camp experience. Pathways and driveways: concrete. Sleeping quarters: concrete. On concrete we showered. On concrete we dined. On concrete we roughhoused, fell and bled. And when the wind gusted up and blew through, concrete formed the base of the mini-dunes that linked craft building to mess hall.

At night we slept four to the room in two bunk beds. Through some lottery (paper/scissors/rock?) I got the top bunk and my year-older cousin Linda the bunk below. Thin and ripe with mildew, those seen-lots-of-kids mattresses; needle sharp, those rusty iron bedsprings. Regardless, I slept so deeply even rolling off and smack-landing on the concrete floor didn't entirely wake me. Climbing back up, I stepped, Linda later told me, on her hair. She pinched my ankle to hurry me along, she said. Since she typically, reflexively, pinched in retaliation, there's no reason to doubt that detail. Of the experience, first to last, I remember only this: I woke where I started, on the top bunk, snuggled in.

To swim in the Croatan Sound meant hiking beyond concrete, through a yaupon grove. Along that patchily shaded trail, we kicked up bits of burning sand and snapped towels at one another, messing around while we could. No horseplay allowed in the water. To keep track of us in the Croatan Sound, the swimming instructor had erected a corkboard with numbers. A number turned "in," toward cork, meant the camper was in the water; number turned "out" meant the camper had returned landside. Before each lesson, the swimming instructor harped on the importance of the check in/check out board while we fidgeted, restrained from diving into water by his authority—but just.

Then came the afternoon when, wrapped in damp towels and queued up in standard Head/Heart/Hands/Health fashion, we counted off and were told to count off again. And again. In all three instances, our numbers were off by one. On the board, we now noticed, a single tag turned inward. In a voice that alarmed us far more than the loner tag, the swimming instructor ordered us into a different kind of line, one that stretched to his left and right, parallel to the water's edge. Arms linked, when told to walk forward, we walked forward. If our fellow camper had drowned and sunk, if that sunken body had snagged on seaweed or other underwater debris, our death chain aimed to free it. The water sloshed around our ankles, then our knees, then our waists. No one joked or whimpered. No one spoke. We walked staring straight ahead instead of looking down—our usual tactic for sidestepping crabs. On that water walk, we prayed to step only on crabs. Until the water reached the shortest camper's neck, we walked and then we turned and sloshed back.

In the end, we dislodged the body of no one young, old, friend or stranger. Hurrying to the bathroom, the missing camper had forgotten to turn her tag. The best of all outcomes, but during the anxious interim, before that best-case scenario had been confirmed, a patch of summer lost its carefree glisten. Lights out, I couldn't have been the only sun-toasted, concrete-scabby 4-H-er afraid to close her eyes, afraid dream would replay the day's trauma and make her feel again the Croatan pressing hard against thigh and shin. Yet whether I counted as one of several scarcely mattered. I had begun shunning sleep at sleep-away camp.

My first bout of agitated wakefulness.
A break in the pattern.
A novelty, an exception.
—Or so I presumed.

My Southern high school was named for a Yankee philanthropist who bought 2,500 acres on an island in the Currituck Sound after World War I because he loved to duck hunt. With his third wife, a Mississippi belle, Joseph Palmer Knapp settled on Mackey Island and together the couple focused on improving county schools, most of which operated without heat, lights or running water and none of which stayed in session for longer than three months each year. The Knapps funded two new schools, three "teacherages" to house instructors, and underwrote a hot lunch program. Before any educational facility in the county bore his name (and only his), Joseph Palmer Knapp had been dead ten years.

During my era at J.P. Knapp High School, the student body, all told, numbered fewer than 180—a yeasty microcosm, 180 teenagers. Athletic, social and scholastic rivalries were supercharged and unrelenting. Classroom intrigue tacked onto locker room intrigue tacked onto lunchroom intrigue. All very exhausting, even for a healthy 16-year-old. Every few weeks or so I simply wore out under the pressure, faked sickness and slept in. I needed those breaks; I needed the oblivion and restoration of sleep. To get what I needed, I probably would have done much worse than lie to my mother, but she spared me the escalation. For reasons of her own, I now perceive, on those mornings when, instead of rising, I burrowed deeper, she did no more than check my forehead before closing the door and leaving me to it.

At UNC-Chapel Hill, while I lived on campus, I lived in Parker Dorm, part of a three-dorm residence college. Innovative for its time, Parker featured four-room suites accessed by an open-air posterior hallway. In theory, all rooms were identical, but in fact night noise divided them, two by two. The front side of the building took the brunt of street noise and panty raider pleas; the backside, the rush and jabber of coeds on the go. Nonetheless, when I closed the books, plumped my pillow and switched off my flower-decaled bedside lamp, I slept as if sedated.

To pay for a flight to Europe and a summer Eurrail pass, spring semester, junior year, I took a job waitressing at The Pines, a dark and cavernous restaurant near the golf course. Frequented by legendary UNC basketball coach Dean Smith, The Pines had cachet. A very efficient pro named Mae tutored me in the unobtrusive gallantries of table hovering and lobster bib distribution. More importantly, she demonstrated how to get through the constantly swinging kitchen door without getting rammed, dropping my tray or bloodying my nose. Expert guidance notwithstanding, I made a wretched waitress—never calm, visibly panicked. The dim lights probably helped to disguise some of the panic, but a total blackout couldn't have concealed all. (In a statistically significant number of diners, server ineptitude must elicit pity. There simply is no other explanation for my tips.) Past 11 p.m., no new customers were seated, regardless of how creatively they tried to bribe the hostess, which meant the staff knocked off after midnight. Any dating I did began after my shift. Maybe, maybe, I turned in by 2:30 a.m. No matter: the instant I *decided* to go to sleep, to sleep I went and stayed in that fair land till morning.

On the European venture, sooner than expected, my tip cache ran short. Booked on a charter flight, I couldn't fly home early without spending more money, so I decided to hole up in a cheap bed and breakfast on the southern coast of England and by other strict economies stretch the funds remaining. For food, I made do with the breakfast provided and a mid-afternoon fruit pie. For entertainment, I walked an overcast beach and read and reread a falling apart copy of *Anna Karenina*, courtesy of a used bookstall in Switzerland. When a book leaves a lasting impression, where I slept and what I dreamed while reading it figures prominently in the recall. *Anna Karenina* logs in thus: English seaside, mahogany bed, snow and lots of it.

And there, in Camber by the Sea, the sleep idyll ends.

Or does it, since the end of an idyll requires there *be* an idyll to end?

Besides being a plague, a scourge and despoiler of equanimity, insomnia turns out to be a naysaying quibbler. It quarrels before it accepts. Just now it's quarreling with previous descriptions of my sleeping past.

Not strictly within the boundaries of accurate is the implication.

Quite possibly a whitewash (if not hogwash).

Very likely delusion dressed up as nostalgia.

Sleep *nostalgia*—that's the charge and defamation of character that shreds my confidence.

And so, again and another: *Sleep, A Personal History.*

Reexamined, my father's sleep composite holds up just fine, I'm pleased to report. It withstands scrutiny, survives the hunt for error and inconsistency, and resists a skeptic's revision. Dubby was a man who loved to sleep and given the opportunity did so without fanfare or difficulty.

Bravo for him.

Alas, Dubby represents only the male side of my formative household.

My first survey shortchanged the distaff.

Never a good idea, in any circumstance, to underrate the female influence.

The women in closest range, my in-house hyper mother and next-door grumpy grandmother, were both chronically sleep-deprived, I now surmise. Several times a week, my mother left bed to sew or iron clothes. An excess of energy, I thought (or was lead to believe). Up with the owls and the roosters, Grandma Dora watched television nonstop in a house trailer moored in a field seeded with grass. Because she was bored, because she was lonely, I assumed. From our kitchen window, her black and white portable appeared to be a floating box of flickering light.

How could I have forgotten that focal point within rural night?

How could I have forgotten Dora in her rocking chair, perpetually awake and crabby?

Another television flashback.

Mom off to her Women's Club meeting, Dad settled in with the newspaper, yours truly planted too close to a broadcast of Walt Disney's "Darby O'Gill and the Little People." Several times I glanced over my shoulder, hoping Dubby would lower the newspaper and say: "Turn it off. Quit watching that nonsense." Instead he kept reading and I kept watching: filmy banshees, headless coachmen, death dolled up and speeding toward thresholds. By the time my mother returned, I was not only afraid to go to bed, I was afraid to leave the living room.

And so began The Year of the Nightlight.

A pink plastic nightlight, it was, with a fiery red switch. Plugged into the outlet next to my bed, the contraption so peculiarly illuminated my own skin I scared myself. Plugged into the outlet near the foot of the bed, it lit up boogeymen. Desperate to elude the nightly monster brigade, I confided in cousin Linda (the pincher), who not only understood my dilemma but had already pre-tested a solution.

Beset by creepy shadows? Name them: Betty, Arnold, Sassafras and Clyde. Summon forth those demons for a chat. ID *them* before they have chance to leap out and terrify you.

Excellent, excellent advice.

That Parker Dorm night noise description? It requires an addendum.

My roommate, a journalism major, was a scholar, activist and campus leader who quickly distinguished herself from her more lackluster, so-called peers. The Valkyries, a prestigious, mysterious campus honor society for women, took note of Brenda's accomplishments and voted her into their ranks. Given the high-drama spookiness of the post-midnight induction ceremony, it would have seemed prudent to alert the inductee's roommate, but perhaps roommates had blabbed before and ruined the surprise.

None the wiser, both Brenda and I turned in for the night.

Before I woke sufficiently to hear and identify the actual gong, I dreamed that unsettling noise coming closer, honing in. Much worse: the real gong replicated my dream gong, beat for ominous beat.

I say I would have appreciated advance warning, but no warning in words could have prepared me for the actuality of five strangers in hooded black robes swooping into my night room brandishing lit candles. As a cluster they moved toward Brenda's bed, then fanned out to surround it. The gonging ceased; the murmuring began; the candles continued to flicker. I can scarcely believe even now that we refrained from serially screaming. Bolt upright, sheets to our necks, spines plastered against headboards, neither of us moved another inch until one of us was instructed to do so. When Brenda got out of bed, the gonging revived. Wearing PJs, hair nesty, she followed that dark entourage out the door and into the night. In the wake of her departure, I didn't turn on a light, didn't dare sleep. Fully awake I was and remained, ears big, eyes bigger, awaiting the return of the snatched.

Also residing in Parker Dorm at the time, the very model of girl and sleep prematurely parted—if only I'd bothered to notice the clues. Weekday and weekend evenings, at or a bit after 10 p.m., honors student Susan in fluffy robe and fluffier slippers settled herself, books, notebooks, pens, pencils, highlighters, paperclips and six-pack of Tab on one of two vinyl sofas in the communal study room. End to end fluorescent lights overhead. Black and white scuffed linoleum underfoot. Institution-green walls and one oversized clock hanging above the single, curtain-less window. In that stark, sterile, echo-y space, hour after hour, Susan studied by her lonesome, clock ticking, fluorescence buzzing, window panes hugging night.

She was very smart, maybe brilliant, that girl in the sleepless lair. She didn't need to study half the night. She just did.

Unrestrained splurging wasn't the reason my money ran short in Europe. I seldom ate in restaurants, stayed mostly in hostels and, to scrimp further on lodging costs, took a lot of overnight trains. Whereas French and German trains zipped along, Spanish trains proceeded at a pace that seemed to extend rather than conquer night. On the train to Barcelona, I shared a compartment with five passengers, some of those snacking to pass the time, others sleeping or faking the checkout. Whenever I closed my eyes and tried to relax into the jiggle and sway, the songster seated next to me leaned over to spit-croon: "Ooo, baby, baby, issa wile world." My Spanish being what it was—pathetically inadequate—I couldn't say *For the love of God, shut up and let me sleep!* Nor could I think of the Cat Stevens equivalency in English. And so the Spanish night wore on, sleep and I separated by song.

It was in Italy, in Florence, that I caught the nasty cold that morphed into chills and fever. Usually ultra-diligent about sticking to my sightseeing schedule, this day I couldn't muster the energy for art or architecture, however majestic. The room I dozed in played host to cots in addition to my own, a portion of a private home having been given over to commerce. After breakfast, the other occupants cleared out for the day. I dozed alone. Local lads perpetually lounged in the front parlor, checking out the foreigners. I didn't hear the door open. I didn't hear the journey, door to cot, but I could identify what jumped on top of me: one of the parlor boys, Victor by name. Victor had the advantage of my recline, wooziness and astonishment; I had the advantage of adrenaline. I got him off. I was neither raped nor near-raped. I kicked; he landed on the floor. Physically Victor did me no harm. Even so, prior to that grope and grab, I had never worried about such a thing happening. After it happened, the fear and expectation of its repetition lived with me, side by side. Darkness and night most especially raised my guard. I couldn't shake the influence. As a result, the Victor incident, the Victor skirmish, radically affected the rest of the trip, Florence through Camber.

My final night abroad I planned to spend dozing on the airport floor. Chatting with another American on the train to Gatwick, I complained about a filched suitcase. I'd left it in an unlocked basement in London. It was my security screw-up, my fault. Nonetheless, a mother and daughter seated nearby overheard my tale of woe and, as recompense, the mother, urged on by the daughter, invited me to spend my last night in their country in their home.

It was an extraordinarily kind and generous offer, both touching and embarrassing. I was sorry they had overheard my whining, sorry to have given the impression that I considered England a land of thieves, very sorry to decline their hospitality. But I couldn't have accepted, not just then. In a stranger's house, however kind the stranger or comfortable the stranger's bed, I wouldn't have been able to sleep. Not a wink.

College prepares; it also, in most cases, postpones the full-bore stresses and worries of adulthood in practice. For my first job, degree in hand, I worked out of a deserted strip mall office from four to eight p.m., scheduling house-call appointments for salesman selling backhoe training courses. As a newly graduated bachelor of arts, before misplacing my talent for sleep altogether, I slept hard to avoid consciousness of an existence no longer punctuated or defined by a classroom. Ten-, twelve-, fourteen-hour sessions by night, multiple catnaps by day, usually in a chair that was losing its stuffing by the fistfuls. To label the self of that period "depressed" doesn't quite cover the symptomatology of my malaise. I was listless, yes, and blue. But I was also stark raving terrified. What if the best already lay behind me? What if one day I woke up from my catnap and decided there was no reason, ever, to leave that decomposing chair?

As we float in our mothers' wombs, three-quarters of our sleep is REM sleep, rapid eye movement sleep, dream sleep. The instant we're born, the REM percentage drops to 50 percent. Once we become adults, another percentage drop, down to 25. During my molting-in-chairs phase, had I known such statistics, I would have scoffed. I would have scoffed louder had anyone suggested to me that I—a snoozing *genius*—would ever lose the knack, the crutch, the comfort, the divine right and trusted escape of instantaneous sleep.

To the marvel and interest of probably no one other than myself, my sleep history precisely mimics the sleep histories of legions of insomniacs. Once upon a time we slept with pleasure. Another once upon a time we slept interrupted. And now, God help us wretches, we sleep hardly at all, left to the torments of capricious night, to parameters of darkness inside of which we feel distraught, undone, powerless, and mythically alone.

Inside of which nothing good seems doable; nothing bad, dodge-able.

Inside of which no solutions exist, only complications subjected to further complication.

Along with some 70 million of my countrywomen and men, I abjectly mourn the lost and profoundly crave the denied. Sleep, that "serious and complete thing" (Robert Penn Warren), that "spirit touching earth" (Nina Berberova), that Shakespearean wonder that "knits up the ravell'd sleeve of care," no longer consumes one third of our existence and the time redistribution is cause for deep, deep sorrow. However much I might wish my situation to be otherwise, the facts of my current condition are these: the want, the need, the *determination* to crawl into bed, close my eyes and sleep until morning simply won't get the job done. To desire is not to achieve or to sustain. Not anymore.

And so, awake, I brood about being awake.

And about circadian rhythms. And melatonin production. And the unwelcome news that caffeine can linger in the body up to 12 hours. "Short sleepers" have higher metabolic rates, heart rates and body temperatures. Short sleepers also consume more oxygen, secrete more cortisol, which translates: *more stressed.* After eight days and nights of staying awake for charity, disc jockey Peter Tripp hallucinated spiders in his shoes. When REM pioneer Nathaniel Kleitman was asked to define the role of sleep, the scientist/philosopher replied: "Tell me what the role of wakefulness is and I will explain the role of sleep." "Pity us! Oh pity us! We wakeful," bemoaned Rudyard Kipling.

Foxes dig up the ground, circle, tamp and circle again before they bed down. Benjamin Franklin favored a well-ventilated bedroom. Someone named Norman Dine filled a fiberglass tub of water, dumped in 25 pounds of salt, heated the mixture to 100 degrees Fahrenheit, eased into that briny bed and tried to sleep afloat. Tuckered out by coup planning, Lenin and Trotsky napped on the floor of the Smolny. Wilbur and Orville Wright pitched a tent in windy, mosquito-plagued Kitty Hawk and forewent rest for the sake of aviation.

Most memorable celluloid insomniac?

David Bowie as the aging, sleepless vampire in the film *The Hunger.*

Best description of a sleepless politico in print?

Woodward and Bernstein's *Final Days* sketch of Richard Nixon, roaming the White House corridors, gibbering at the presidential portraits.

Who among the famous and infamous *should* have slept badly before which life-altering event (even if, in fact, they slept like bats)?

- Bugsy Siegel, after his mob cronies met in Havana.
- Andrew Borden, stretched on his living room couch, August 4, 1892.
- Ted Hughes, after Assia Wevill came to lunch in Devon.
- Ernest Simpson, before the English Midlands house party that introduced wife Wallis to Edward, Prince of Wales.
- Ditto the above for Edward, Prince of Wales.
- Patty Hearst, before that knock on her Berkeley door, 1974.
- Lev Davidovich Bronstein, before allowing Ramon Mercader into his Coyoacán study.
- Anna Akhmatova, before composing "In Praise of Peace" in "repentance."

You get the gist. And if you are an insomniac, you've played this tired and futile game.

Neighbor Trim, Also Awake

Of course Trim is not his mama-given, birth-recorded name. Officially, he's a William, same as his daddy, his daddy's daddy, his son and who knows how many others dangling from the branches of the Smithson family tree. Regardless, once this particular William "shot up," nobody (birth mother included) called him anything but Trim, shunning namesake traditions in favor of nicknaming according to the look of a beast. On the country road turned state road alongside which Trim grew up and continues to reside, his neighbor Stumpy came to be known as Stumpy because of an exaggeratedly short neck. As can be surmised, Trim was trim. Started trim, stayed trim. It's a lanky man who stretches on the Barcalounger, one light of a three-light pole lamp illuminating his kneecap, the rest of him and that late-night room effaced by shadow as the earth spins round and round and round.

I'm not peeping in Trim's window. I'm projecting, one coast to another, his kinswoman in wide awake. I know the kind of night that eddies up against the solitary. I know how darkness can turn claustrophobic. I'm familiar with the melancholies of sleeplessness. The man has my sympathy in some respects—not all.

Many times, from many sources, I've heard how Trim "locks himself up" inside his house at night; how any driver taking the night loop, Shawboro to Sligo, Sligo to Shawboro, sees, despite the drawn shades, the leakage of illumination that *proves* Trim's "in there watching that smut that got him in trouble in the first place."

Porn on cable, they mean. Simulated sexual gymnastics via satellite dish.

About that watching, about Trim's engagement with the broadcast in progress: somehow I can't quite envision a riveted Trim. I can believe he's half watching, maybe as little as a quarter watching. I can believe he's pointed toward a TV screen, eyes trained in the direction of that image flash. But the viewer himself? Animated? Revved to the point of jack off? I have my doubts.

In serving the cause of a Southern Baptist morality tale, nothing bests weaknesses of the flesh, but I'm inclined to blame Trim's woes on loneliness because for the last 15 years or more that loneliness has been manifest. He feeds, and refuses to have neutered, a mongrel pack of dogs, a multiplying base of companion curs. He clips his box shrubs and mows his "skint to dirt" lawn several times a week. Long before his clapboard house has begun to weather, Trim is up on his stepladder, scraping, priming, but also glancing around, using his paintbrush to wave and hail and flag down anyone willing to stop and jaw.

Trim's original, benign reputation reflected a gift for gab, but now, according to Shawboro opinion, both the man and his reputation have "gone astray," a process that has been episodic (in incident) and cumulative (in harms done).

In summary: he publicly threatened his ex-wife with a rifle. He quarreled and broke with both his children, a son and a daughter. He quit his upholstery business. He sold off several parcels of inherited land. At the age of 68, he was arrested and accused of fondling two teenaged girls. Convicted of those crimes, he announced he had throat cancer and hovered "at death's door." Then he announced a miraculous cure. "One hundred percent cancer-free."

"That Trim," many people have said on many occasions. "You cain't listen to Trim."

Nevertheless, the Dubby Meads family listened to neighbor Trim, welcomed the diversion of listening to him, the evening he came to pay his respects to the dead. Freshly bathed and shaved, crewcut oiled and glistening, he started talking on the front steps, slug slow and backwoods twangy, telling my brother and me what a fine neighbor our father had always been in times flush and troubled.

"When Billy shot your dog, any other man in Shawboro would have held it against him and me," Trim said, referring in the first instance to his son, in the second to Dubby. "But your daddy, your daddy didn't hold it against us. I wanted to get you another dog but he wouldn't hear of that either. Said: 'Trim, your boy didn't mean to kill the dog. Nobody's holding him to blame.'"

If my father did say that, he fibbed. *I* held Billy responsible, as did my mother.

"Who shoots under a dark house when a dog's in heat?" she asked when it happened, incredulous, incensed.

"That's just the kind of man your daddy was," Trim told Dubby's two children on Dubby's front steps, February 1985. "Never treated me or Billy any different. Never once."

When grief combines with shock, a person can go through the motions required of her and still be in a fugue state. I was in a fugue state. I knew Trim was talking and I was hearing him talk on that unseasonably mild February night but for all intents and purposes I had succumbed to time warp, reverted to the kid I'd been, devastated by the death of a pet, not a parent, standing alongside my mother, facing neighbors Trim and Billy, come expressly to our front steps to apologize.

And Trim saying to Billy: "Go on, now. Say what you've come to say."

And Billy saying: "I didn't mean it. I'm sorry. I didn't mean to hit your dog. I was just trying to run him off."

And Trim saying: "Let me get you another one. Whatever kind of dog you want, you just name it and I'll find one. Puppy or grown. You just tell me what you want."

And my wanting my dead dog and only the dead, not an inadequate replacement, crying because I recognized the futility of that wish, all wanting aside.

And while I cried and leaned against my mother's hip and Billy held his elbows and hung his head, Trim talked and talked, trying to make amends that couldn't be made. That morning, startlingly so, the sky stayed blue and the grass stayed green despite my dead dog, just as on that winter night in 1985, the moon shone and the swamp sang without my father there to see or hear.

Invited in, Trim extended his condolences to my mother, then settled himself, arm stretched across the back of the couch, head cocked to the side, free, after acknowledging our sorrow, to reminisce about happier times. Dubby and Trim had grown up within sprinting distance of each other and when they married built homes and started families in closer proximity, on Meads and Smithson family land, respectively. They'd been country boys together, amusing themselves in country boy fashion, swinging naked from swamp vines, attempting to drive borrowed roadsters across canal beds. Clearly enjoying the reverie, Trim told tales on my father, my uncles, himself. "I remember that time your Uncle Carl was drivin'. Flipped me right out of the backseat. I tell you what, I hit the dirt running, did that. Peelt the skin right off the soles of my feet," Trim regaled, and my brother and I laughed, relieved to be reminded that there remained a past safe and inviolate, unthreatened by oblivion, immune to take away. Neither winded nor sleepy, tireless Trim talked on and on. If we hadn't eventually turned him out, I suspect he would have stayed on our couch, spinning tales till night acquiesced to day.

Back on the steps, drawing out his departure, he said: "I'll tell your mama later, but right now I'm telling you. Anything she needs and I can help her with, I'm right down the road, happy to do it. And if she needs something done and I cain't do it, I'll find her somebody that can. Your daddy would do anything for a neighbor and wouldn't take no money for it neither. You tell your mama I plan on doing the same for her."

My brother and I thanked him for the offer, thanked him for coming by, both of us fairly certain our mother wouldn't be calling on Trim to help with a clogged drain or flat tire. She'd go to certified family first. Nonetheless we appreciated the sentiment and its charity. Trim would have helped out our mother if she needed help, if she asked. She just wouldn't ask.

An example of the kind of seized upon and senseless calculating that keeps me awake while others sleep: if I waved to Trim every time I left the house in Shawboro, as a kid, as a teenager, as a visiting adult, how many times in my lifetime had I waved to Trim?

Even as a kid, walking to the bus or to the mailbox or riding by on my bike, I knew to put some speed on, crossing Trim territory. He'd yak at a child as soon as he would an adult. He'd talk about his yard or garden or dogs. He'd ask after my grandmother, her yard, her garden. He'd tell you exactly who that hour had come and gone along Meads Road by bike, tractor and car. He'd ask about my plans for the rest of the morning or afternoon, update me on his kids' doings. He'd chat about weather, yellow flies, the quality of the crops in the field across the way. Any topic you mentioned he'd latch onto and run to ground, conversationally. Never the first to break off any exchange, he'd discuss shoestrings for five minutes if you didn't turn heel and flee.

Rather than calculating the number of times I'd waved at Trim, I should have been mulling the reason Trim was so often at home in the middle of the day even back when I was a kid and he was gainfully employed, married and the practicing father of two. His business wasn't failing or threatened with failure. By local standards, it counted as a smashing success. In addition to Shawboro clientele, he did upholstery work for the Camden crowd and a percentage of the Elizabeth City trade. At one time or other, he refurbished every one of our living room chairs and probably did the same for the majority of Shawboro households. He also reupholstered car seats to rave reviews: "Looks 'xactly like new. No one'd ever guess it'd been redone." The only mini-threat to Trim's business monopoly, short-lived, came from the Shawboro Women's Club. For one of their winter projects, under the direction of the Home Extension agent, members were taught the rudiments of chair upholstery. My mother carted to the Community Building the rocker in which she had sung lullabies to both her babies. Not at all satisfied with the results of her own handiwork, she called in the professional. Trim came to the house, measured; they discussed and chose a fabric (based less on beauty than durability), and the chair survives today in Trim's version of revamp.

I was still short enough to stand on the front seat of the family's '51 Ford when Dubby quit the Ford Plant in Norfolk, Virginia, to work as an electrician for Shelton Simpson. Trim's wife, Eva, also worked in Shelton's Shawboro appliance store in the dual role of bookkeeper/receptionist. Having a job outside the home made Eva unusual among Shawboro women. Since Trim's upholstery shop prospered, their family didn't absolutely need a second income. During that era, Shawboro wives and mothers toiled outside the home to help keep their family in clothes, food and shelter, not to prevent themselves from going mad. If Dubby hadn't quite finished for the day when we arrived to collect him, Mom parked the Ford and visited with Eva.

Like her husband, Eva talked slow. Unlike Trim, she drawled more than she twanged. "Hayyyyyy," she'd say. "How ya dooooo-in?" She worked eight to five at a metal desk alongside Shelton's display stock of General Electric appliances. While Eva and my mother chatted, I skipped up and down the row, opening refrigerator and oven doors to ogle the plaster of Paris food inside. Green beans, yellow corn, a ring of biscuits, a slab of ham, a full-sized "cooked" turkey, waxy brown. Eva surely noticed the coveting because once Christmas rolled around Dubby brought home the lot, beans to turkey. For years I played with those blocks of painted food. Years. The paint chipped, the edges cracked and crumbled, and still I laid that bounty on my make-believe dinner table in my mostly make-believe playhouse—straw for rugs, sticks for doors and pine cones for decoration.

When Shelton retired and closed up shop, Eva took the civil service exam. Initially she assisted my Aunt Vivian in the post office. After Aunt Vivian also called it quits, Eva took over as head post mistress. Standard wisdom in Shawboro: you couldn't do better than a civil service job. Good benefits, good pension and, as post mistress, half a day free every Saturday. When Eva left Trim, she didn't ask him for money. She'd accumulated enough on her own.

Eva's decision to leave seemed to shock the community as much as the abandoned husband. Couldn't believe it, never saw it coming.

"Just beside himself," the stunned said of the stunned Trim. "Talks of nothing else."

In quick succession Trim quarreled with his son (who took his mother's side) and with his daughter (less partisan). He quit the upholstery business and dissolved the father/son partnership. He began to spend not just a portion of his days but all day every day at home, aggrieved, sulking, blaming one woman for that unhappy manner of being. He upped his grass mowing to every other day and then, one afternoon, grass shorn to the nub, he took his rifle and headed for the post office.

The post office in Shawboro, as in any small community, is a social hub where more than mail gets picked up. To spark-fire gossip, Trim couldn't have chosen a better locale to threaten his wife of record. A trip to the post office might take 10 minutes or 30, depending on who else bought stamps or loitered in the parking lot. The afternoon Trim and his gun made their appearance, there were several Shawborians on the scene, natives who knew Trim and didn't in ordinary circumstances fear him. But on this occasion, besides looking as if he'd given up sleeping, he looked wild in the eye and jittery in the hand.

Not a promising combination: a loaded gun and jittery.

Those unlucky enough to find themselves at the post office with Trim realized fairly quickly—and no doubt with accelerating alarm—that he was "in a state" and unlikely to respond to reasoning. I would also guess that some of those observers started shimmying toward the door before Trim "took it into his head" that he wanted community reps to hear what he had to say to Eva—witnesses in Trim's mind, hostages as viewed by the law. Since he hadn't locked or otherwise barricaded the door, other unsuspecting souls wandered in to join the witness/hostage pool, including the preacher of Providence Baptist Church who, Monday through Saturday, drove to the post office to pick up his personal mail and the church's mail in a two-for-one run. Once inside, the preacher saw Trim primarily pointing a rifle at Eva behind the counter but also swinging the barrel in other directions, which meant that the preacher found himself negotiating to save God's children in a context other than church, on a day other than Sunday. The preacher, Eva, or the preacher and Eva working in tandem, must have succeeded in calming the stressed because no one got shot point blank or grazed during the standoff. After an hour or so, Trim agreed to surrender both himself and weapon to the authorities.

"Once they got him out of there, truth told, he looked right pitiful," it was said of Trim, a man who'd lost his wife, the support of his children and after that stunt the respect of most of his community, Dubby gone and fewer and fewer of those who remained inclined to treat Trim "no different."

Trim blamed medication for the boil up of emotion. "Confused in my head. Dwellin' on grievance," he told anyone who'd listen.

Eva took out a restraining order, hired a better lawyer, got a quicker than scheduled divorce and set up house in Elizabeth City, ten miles distant from

Trim and his firearms. A self-protective move, a wise decision, but it left her ex-husband at looser ends.

When I visited home, post-Eva and Trim split, to get to the house my mother also lived in solo, I had to drive past Trim's. The grass stayed skint, the hedges clipped, the shutters painted, but Trim sightings became something of a rarity. He must have undertaken his mowing and painting near dawn or twilight because he no longer hung out in the yard the way he used to in the bright of day. No question he was in residence. His truck was parked in the driveway, its tires leaned on by curs, staring back at the starers who passed.

Following the post office incident, perhaps out of pity, his daughter attempted a reconciliation that didn't stick. Son Billy kept to his no-contact policy, that cut-off, in time, taking on a whiff of self-righteousness. People understood the whys and wherefores of Billy's position and hostility, but his prolonged shunning of Trim didn't endear him to the community. A father is a father. A son is a son. Ever after, evermore, regardless. To a Southerner, that's an unshakable fundamental.

So Trim was left with his dogs, his Barcalounger, his satellite dish, empty days and emptier nights. Eventually he paid a 42-year-old Walnut Island resident, Glenda Marline Harley, to bring in company: first an 18-year-old female, then a 16-year-old female.

The "nature of the offenses involved mostly fondling. Sexual intercourse was not performed," Currituck County Sheriff Susan Johnson told the Elizabeth City *Daily Advance*, leaving *Advance* readers, including Trim's former wife, son, daughter and neighbors, to speculate whether that failure of penetration resulted from lack of interest or lack of member ability. Also unreported: the amount Trim paid his procurer. Glenda Marline Harley was, in any case, of little interest to the Shawboro contingent of Trim watchers and commentators. An accomplice, a co-conspirator in sexual transgression perhaps, but a secondary character in the unfolding Saga of Trim.

"Who's this Glenda Harley?" Trim's neighbors inquired of one another in a tone of don't much care.

"Never heard the name."

"Must not be from around here."

"Must not."

Nothing beyond that give and take was required to terminate the topic of Glenda Marline Harley, wherever and however she had made the acquaintance of native citizen Trim.

It was the 16-year-old who notified the police. And it was the 16-year-old's complaint that led to the investigation that led to charges of two counts of second-degree forcible sex, one count of promoting prostitution of a minor, and one count of performing a crime against nature.

All of the above occurred during the month of March. March is a bleak month in eastern North Carolina, spring promised but spring denied. Shawborians go a little stir crazy in March; they ride the roads, on the hunt for buds, blossoms and cloud breaks in an overcast sky. If they have to use the car or truck heater to take the chill off during those expeditions, they gripe and grumble.

"Havin' to run the heater. And here it is March."

"In both cases," the *Daily Advance* reported, "Harley was either driving past or taking the girls somewhere else when she made up an excuse to stop at Smithson's house in rural Shawboro."

Was the heater on in Harley's car?

I wonder.

Was the TV on in Trim's house?

I wonder that too.

But that's as far as I'll follow the wonder in a scenario involving two teenaged girls locked in with 68-year-old Trim.

Convicted on all counts, Trim eluded jail but not an ankle monitor. Given the man's habits, house arrest couldn't have imposed too great a restriction. To keep his client out of jail, Trim's lawyer argued ill health and Trim followed up that successful plea with the throat cancer bulletin that presaged the cure bulletin that resuscitated the Shawboro refrain:

"That Trim. You cain't listen to Trim."

Trim Smithson, his trials and tribulations, wouldn't commingle with my night broods if I didn't connect the loss I mourn above all others with one of his own. When my father died, Trim was stripped of a different kind of baseline comfort: a tolerant, forgiving friend.

Tell you what though, as they say in Shawboro. If I were Trim, I'd be glad Dubby Meads hadn't been around to hear a 16-year-old testify about sexual coercion behind a locked door in his neighbor's home. I'd be thankful the man expired before his friendship.

The Rise and Fall of Sheriff Glenn Brinkley

This is the advantage of receiving updates on the lives of childhood companions: you get the long view.

This is the disadvantage of receiving updates on the lives of childhood companions: you get the long view.

Why amuse/torment the self with retrospective tabulations of progress or lack thereof?

Ask that question and you aren't now nor have you ever been an insomniac.

From 1994 to 2000, Glenn Everett Brinkley served as the top law officer of Currituck County, North Carolina, "Land of the Wild Goose," "Sportsman's Paradise," coastal Carolina farmland turned developer wet dream. Biological son of "Big Earl," Ford Plant employee, and Jean, hardworking nurse, Glenn counted as a charter member of my Shawboro kid pack. Also: my first-grade boyfriend and second-grade valentine.

During the summers, little else to occupy the time, I and my Shawboro cronies rode bikes for hours. On dirt roads, field paths, into tractor gullies and drainage ditches, we pedaled until we came to a cow fence. And then we got off and hefted first the bikes, then ourselves, over the obstruction. Lift, toss, scramble—that was the scheme. But how like insomnia to fixate on the point of challenge: kids grunting and heaving ad infinitum, Glenn grunting and heaving.

Back when, we gave the boy credit for doggedness, if little else. Guaranteed: none of Glenn's classmates, teachers, coaches or guidance counselors took him for an up and comer. If ambitious to succeed, he hid it well. He didn't excel at schoolwork; he'd failed a grade. He didn't excel at sports; his athletic prowess ranged, depending on the game, from average to a fraction below. He wasn't a student leader; no teacher made him her pet. He accumulated enough credits to graduate, but at commencement won no awards, not even for citizenship. There were no clues, not one, of big things on the horizon for sheriff-to-be Glenn.

Glenn's response to his mama's supper call, according to my cousin Chris's memory, was this: "I'll be there in three or two minutes."

"Three or two minutes," repeats my cousin, shaking his head in the manner of the deeply pitying.

On such tics, reputations are built, dry and calcify in Currituck County. And yet, flabbergasting those who knew him young, grown-up Glenn got himself twice elected sheriff. For six tough years, he preserved the peace, protected the good folk, hunted down the bad, wore proudly a gut-restraining uniform the color of dung and fulfilled the duties and obligations Currituck County voters and residents had entrusted him to fulfill. Then came the otherwise unexceptional day an 11-year-old girl in custody spat in his face and to that mucus provocation Sheriff Glenn responded as a law officer untrained in dealing with the newly apprehended.

Six years, one moment.

Six years of restraint undone by a single unchecked impulse.

In outline, in its broad strokes, in the majority of its middling and not so middling incidentals, Glenn's is a Southern tale, Southern to the core.

During our Valentine swapping days, Glenn and his family lived in a rented house five houses east of the central Shawboro crossroads. A two-story house lacking shutters, plain to the point of austerity. While Jean Brinkley nursed others, Coreen Brinkley, eldest child and only daughter, looked after her three brothers. Blindly partial to her siblings, Coreen took their side utterly and regardless on any issue, in any circumstance, against anyone, adult or child. If she suspected someone of mistreating the boys, she took on the offense as her own.

"Acts just like a mother hen," Shawboro said of Coreen—a compliment, not a criticism.

When finances improved, the Brinkleys moved into a larger house, three lots closer to Shawboro's center, previously owned by my great aunt Hattie Barnard. During her residence, Great Aunt Hattie favored a back room that looked and felt crepuscular at high noon. Long ready to be done with this world, she spent her days in a rocking chair, desultorily flicking a folding fan. Should visitors intrude, she suffered their presence with eyes firmly closed. The Brinkleys brought commotion and spirit back to a dwelling that sorely needed the boost. Like his brothers and sister, Glenn lived in his parents' house, with his parents, until he married.

Glenn's first wife, a down-county gal, was also his high school honey.

From the onset of their togetherness, Sandra knew which of Glenn's buttons to push and when. There were many, many tortured breakups and reconciliations. More than once Glenn pled for his beloved's forgiveness in the lunchroom line. He was by no means an imaginative suitor, but he was a persistent pursuer and convincingly stricken when dumped. The breakups clearly distressed him more than her. Nonetheless, in the final accounting, it was Glenn who got what he wanted. Sandra agreed to become Mrs. Brinkley—with a marked lack of enthusiasm, it must be said, but still she agreed.

So: a victory for suitor Glenn.

By the time Currituck County elected him chief law enforcement officer, Glenn and Sandra had divorced, he'd remarried and fathered another set of kids. Wife number two was a "young thing," as my people are apt to say when the age difference exceeds a decade. Since I've not had the pleasure of meeting the second Mrs. Brinkley, before or after Glenn's power heyday, I'm in no position to make comparative judgments. But if the second Mrs. Brinkley has somehow managed to retain her youthful looks, she has certainly beaten the odds. Worry, humiliation and malicious gossip tend to age a woman—as does a husband who, within the space of a year, suffers a career meltdown and heart attack, real or staged.

Land.

In Currituck County, land simultaneously qualifies as sacred, a ticket "up," the stuff of legacy and the stuff of feuds.

Under the sheriff's jurisdiction: 443.63 square miles of county, 261.4 of which is solid ground, the remainder waterways and marshland. Although most of Currituck is contiguous, two sizeable sections are not. The section called Currituck Outer Banks is separated from the mainland by the Currituck Sound. To reach the Currituck Outer Banks, a sheriff or ordinary citizen must drive down county, cross the bridge at Point Harbor, then steer north, through Dare County's Southern Shores and Duck. Even without the bumper-to-bumper beach traffic that starts late spring and extends through early fall, policing the Currituck Outer Banks is a logistical nightmare. Also on the sheriff's watch: Knotts Island, accessible by ferry or by driving north across the Virginia state line, through the settlement of Gibbs Woods and bearing south.

According to the North Carolina Department of Commerce, Economic Policy and Research Division, Currituck County is now officially considered part of the Hampton Roads/Virginia Metropolitan Statistical Area (MSA). Depending on which county resident you're conversing with, that bureaucratic linkage counts as a benefit or a liability. Almost two million people call Hampton Roads home. On occasion, a percentage of those scoot across the state line to dump a body or rob a convenience store. Unchecked development notwithstanding, compared to high-density Norfolk or Chesapeake or Newport News, Currituck County still offers a variety of places to lose a corpse: marshes, ditches, drainage canals, patches of deserted woodland and miles of swamp.

History as destiny.

The first federal census, conducted in 1790, recorded 5,219 Currituck inhabitants. Not reflected in that tally: the bandits and thieves living in the Dismal Swamp. An ideal sanctuary for scofflaws, the swamp's density and apparent sameness flummoxed many a lawman. For those who had mastered the art of getting in and out without mishap, however, life was sweet. Swamp denizens regularly raided nearby plantations for food and cattle, then disappeared back from whence they came. Historical precedent, one might argue, for a rebellious and untamed citizenry.

For more than a century and a half, the population of Currituck remained sparse and stable. The 1950 census exceeded the 1790 count by a mere thousand. In 1960, when Glenn and I and our bike buddies roamed, there were still, all told, fewer than 7,000 county residents. The county of Glenn's childhood, of my childhood, resembled the county our parents had known as children much more than it would resemble the boom county of generation next. We'd already traded in bikes for cars before the first of the farmers, unable to sustain a family of four on profits from corn and soybeans, started selling off parcels to developers with intentions to further subdivide.

In many ways, Glenn and I and our contemporaries count as the last of the Currituck provincials.

The economic and cultural shift, when it happened, how it happened, is not of minor importance in the narrative of Sheriff Glenn Brinkley. In a retro community, Glenn's was a retro-to-the-max sensibility. As a young boy and as a teenager, his character remained unvaryingly, transparently this: slow on the uptake, tenacious once decided. Nothing I heard or read about Glenn Brinkley, the adult, the sheriff, suggested a change in that approach or sensibility. Glenn's deep-down notion of Currituck was of a county where kids rode bikes through fields and ditches without supervision or threat of harm. No matter how many dumped bodies he'd seen, the idea that his own children could not bike in similar fashion, without fear or restriction, would, I believe, stick in Glenn's craw, would represent a situation he sought to "correct." Which would mean Glenn Brinkley perceived his mission as sheriff, at least in part, as a campaign to turn back time.

The county's seventeenth sheriff and I both grew up under the governance of sheriff number 15, Luther Sanderlin, who served for 12 years and retired from office in 1972. Never to be glimpsed hatless, Mr. Luther negotiated this world in a body shaped like Tweedledee/dum. Soft-spoken, deliberate, he preferred to settle disputes, whether petty or life threatening, through mediation and calm negotiation. Once and only once, all other options exhausted, he shot a fleeing criminal in the leg. Mr. Luther long courted Annie Sivals. When he died, a bachelor, he left Annie his property and the rest of his possessions. Before he died, when he became ill, Annie took him into her home and nursed him, but only after she'd also asked her sister to move in to avoid any talk of impropriety.

Mr. Luther kept the peace without assistance. His successor, Norman Newbern Jr., felt the need to hire three able-bodied deputies, Glenn one of the three. During that change-over era, my cousin Chris entertained himself by hanging out at the Sheriff's Office, where he overheard Mr. Luther congratulate Norman Jr. on his choice of associates. By hiring the "biggest thief in the county," Mr. Luther said, Norman Jr. could keep a close eye on the sticky-fingered. By hiring a hothead who feared nothing and no one, he gained a front man in situations where a sheriff hesitates to lead by example. And then, for balance, there was Glenn, a fellow who "took awhile to understand things."

"Yep," says cousin Chris, still amused by Mr. Luther's analysis 30 years after its utterance. "Corrupt, crazy and dumb. That was Norman Jr.'s backup."

Last laugh or at least intermediate laugh goes to Glenn. Of Norman Jr.'s deputy triumvirate, only Glenn ran for and was twice elected sheriff, succeeding his former boss in 1994 and winning reelection in 1998, "hard-fought" campaigns both, according to Elizabeth City's *Daily Advance.*

On the campaign trail, Glenn begged votes door to door.

Twice he drove up a driveway he'd once used as a platform for his bike wheelies to ask for my mother's vote. On both occasions she stopped him before he could get out of the car—a county-provided vehicle, second go-around.

"Honey, don't even bother asking," she says she said. "You've got my vote."

If Glenn had run a third time, scandal or no, my mother most probably would have assured him of the same. When I asked why she voted for Glenn, she said: "Well, my lord, I've known the boy since he wore short pants."

And there it be, in a nutshell: if you've known the boy in short pants, how can you abandon the man in long pants? Glenn was homegrown; he didn't stink of Johnny-Come-Lately.

In 1994, when I asked cousin Linda, a middle school administrator, whether she supported Glenn's initial bid for office, she deliberated before answering.

"I'm not sure Glenn can handle the job" was her ultimate assessment. "The county's not like it was."

Overcrowded schools and roadways, scads of out-of-state retirees watching TV in doublewides. A new county water system. County landfills. Prohibitions against burning garbage in oil drums, against tossing worn-out appliances into the woods. Dirt roads paved and signed. Farmhouses, every house, numbered because the latest crew of rescue squad workers and volunteer firefighters didn't know everybody, where they lived and how to get there. Shiny prefab gift shops, seafood restaurants and rest stops alongside pig pens, field graves and barns writ with scripture. New blood and bloodlines, new "input" challenging "the old ways." Transplants who had to be welcomed and accommodated without alienating the native daughters and sons—a delicate balancing act for craftier men than Glenn. And yet he passed muster with a sufficient number of voters on either side of the divide to twice defeat his opponents. He was two years into his second four-year term when the 11-year-old Knotts Island girl, handcuffed to the bars of a jail cell, feet shackled, spat on him and Glenn responded by twice slapping, with an open palm, the spitter on the chest—a reaction that, in and of itself, incorporates a bit of the old and the new. Slow to understand/slow to act Glenn had obviously speeded up with the times. But that sailing wad of disrespect? That wet insult would have infuriated Glenn Brinkley age 8, 12, 26, 39 or 83.

An inveterate snipper of newspaper clippings, my mother typically collects a manila envelope's worth before mailing the batch off to me. She sends any article that mentions relatives, friends, and/or the children of relatives and friends, kinship clarifications added in her handwriting along the margins. She sends wedding announcements, award notices, news of community activism, job promotions, obituaries, arrests, citations for public drunkenness and bankruptcy notices.

Altogether, a mixed bag of Currituck County's faltering and prospering.

Once the slapping news hit the papers, however, the clipping stream,

Carolina to California, contained only articles about "Glenn's troubles," as my mother called the beginning of the end for Sheriff Glenn, and she sent a stack weekly—Glenn's first negative press.

Throughout his initial term as sheriff, he seems to have made a habit of speaking off-the-cuff to reporters without ill effect. In January of 1997, he applauded himself for orchestrating the seizure of 92 pounds of marijuana, "the biggest bust that Currituck County has ever had." He repeatedly blamed Virginia for the county's drug trade. "We're too close to the (state) line," he told the *Virginian-Pilot*. "We're prime." Because the perpetrators of an Eagle's Supermarket robbery in April 1996 "weren't wearing any masks," the sheriff surmised that they weren't, couldn't be, "local people." Also in 1996, Glenn publicly feuded with the high school principal, who had written a letter of support for a parent once convicted of selling crack cocaine. The sheriff viewed this as "interference." In Glenn's view, the parent's sentence (40 hours community service and a $400 fine, plus court fees) had been far too lenient. "You try to do your best," Glenn bitched to a *Virginian-Pilot* reporter, "and you get people writing good letters about something they know nothing about."

In time, Sheriff Glenn learned to watch his words more carefully when conversing with the fourth estate. After two of his deputies threatened at gunpoint the wife of an assistant district attorney and she, in turn, sued the Sheriff's Office for a compensatory $1.5 million to cover "emotional distress, extreme fright, ridicule, embarrassment, humiliation, loss of esteem, anxiety, trauma, stress (and) lost enjoyment of life," Glenn ducked reporters and when found declined comment.

Good prep, that clam-up because deputies aiming pistols at a local attorney's wife didn't begin to compare to the firestorm the sheriff brought down on his department, his subordinates, his family, friends, supporters and himself by slapping, in front of spectators, a handcuffed, leg-shackled kid, October 22, 1999.

Guy Seiderman was one of the deputies who responded when a concerned citizen called to report a Knotts Island girl running through the neighborhood, "wielding an ax." A kid with a "history of mental problems," the *Daily Advance* subsequently reported, much of that history on file at the county Department of Social Services. Tracked and trapped by sheriff's men, the culprit didn't willingly surrender. She had to be rushed and cornered. In custody and cuffed, she was driven back to the mainland for processing. In and out of the squad car, she continued to kick, scream and swear, behavior that resulted in leg restraints as well as handcuffs. Sometime during the latter stages of that uncompromising resistance, the sheriff joined the fracas.

Deputy Seiderman testified that before the spitter spat on the sheriff, she threatened to do precisely that. Glenn, according to Seiderman, countered her threat with one of his own: "You do and you'll see what happens."

She did and what happened, again according to Seiderman's account: "Sheriff Brinkley hit her. I saw it. Other officers know this, and they know the department is trying to shut me up because I saw it and told the truth."

The State Bureau of Investigation conducted a six-month inquiry into the incident and, in the spring of 2000, handed over a 500-page report to the state Attorney General's Office for a ruling on whether or not criminal charges should be filed against Glenn and against Deputy James Lantz for conspiring with the boss to obstruct justice. Following his SBI testimony, Guy Seiderman joined the Army. He told reporters he had been harassed and bullied (slashed tires, intimidating phone calls) and that he feared for his life.

"I don't feel safe (in Currituck)," he said.

And the sheriff? How did he feel?

Stressed, certainly. Stress that precipitated what some in Currituck called a heart attack without adjectival addition, what others labeled a "mild" heart attack, what another set deemed an opportune heart attack, and what yet another bunch dismissed altogether as a sham medical crisis.

At least one someone concluded: "He's just hiding out in the hospital. That's what he's doing."

In the room with me to hear that conclusion voiced, perhaps a dozen Currituckians. None saw fit to argue.

Once released from the hospital, Glenn announced his resignation for health reasons. To fill the void at the top created by that resignation, he appointed his administrative assistant, Susan Johnson, "chief deputy," conferring upon her the power and authority to run the department. Although Johnson soon became a certified law enforcement officer, when appointed she was not. The cynics accused the ex-sheriff of "place holding," of intending to run again for sheriff once the controversy died down, of assuming that should he choose to run again he would, of course, defeat a *woman*, whether or not she proved ingrate enough to challenge his bid for reelection.

About those rumors and innuendos, Glenn issued no public statements, either in rebuttal or support. By September, quashing or encouraging speculation about a return to office couldn't have rated very high on Glenn's must-do list. A grand jury had indicted him and charged the retired sheriff with assault.

In the wake of Glenn's resignation, Susan Johnson was unanimously appointed sheriff by the Board of Commissioners, the first female in county history to hold the post. Neither her title nor the trailblazing spared her the discomfort of having to testify at her former boss's trial.

Tentative, conflicted, part support, part denunciation, the testimony of Susan Johnson.

On the stand, the former administrative assistant admitted that when her superior told her about the slap, she assured him that the adolescent in custody "deserved" the reprimand. She also stated that she had never seen anyone, adult or child, handcuffed and shackled to the jail cell—a disturbing experience. When she noticed the girl's hands "losing color," she became concerned, she said, and asked a deputy to loosen the restraints.

Glenn's jury of peers included a father who admitted to backhanding his son after that son spat on him, a receptionist, a homemaker, a licensed mortician, an electrician, a house cleaner and two department store managers.

Glenn's attorney didn't deny the slap, only its premeditation.

"It was a knee-jerk reaction," he argued and left the grandstanding to the prosecution.

The prosecuting attorney compared the handcuff and shackle restraints to torture methods employed in the Middle Ages. To strike a "defenseless" girl "is an absolute no-no," he told the jury, then accused the ex-sheriff of "violat(ing) the law he was sworn to uphold."

The dramatic, take-the-moral-high-ground summation apparently failed to impress. Following four hours' deliberation, the jury voted to acquit. The editors of the *Daily Advance*, among others, declared the verdict a travesty.

"If Wednesday's jury verdict in ex-Sheriff Glenn Brinkley's assault trial is any indication of how the average Currituck resident thinks a disobedient child should be disciplined, local child abuse investigators may need to consider setting up a special task force there…. (T)he words *outrageous* and *nonsensical* seem to fall short of describing the jury's verdict."

About Glenn's fate, cousin Chris said: "It wasn't the slapping; it was the cover-up that ruined him."

About that spitfire girl, cousin Linda said: "She was a holy terror. The teachers couldn't control her. No one could."

After the verdict came in, when talking to the press, ex-Sheriff Glenn Brinkley kept his remarks short and simple: "I'm glad it's over," he said.

The trial, perhaps, but that was hardly the sum of it.

Most of the citizens of Currituck seemed happy enough with Susan Johnson's ongoing performance as replacement sheriff. Happy enough, not thrilled. Once the ex-sheriff had been acquitted and issued a clean bill of health, a well-organized few lobbied hard for his return to office. By that date Glenn had mastered at least the rudiments of spin. When contacted by the *Daily Advance*, he said he had no plans to run again for sheriff; that he intended to "relax" and "spend time with (his) family."

Boilerplate denials.

A message in code.

Although Glenn wasn't *instantly* throwing his hat back into the ring, he was keeping that hat within easy reach.

One former colleague decidedly not backing Glenn's return to office was Commissioner Eldon Miller, frankly skeptical that anything ex-Sheriff Brinkley said today would remain valid tomorrow.

"Glenn is unpredictable," Miller told the *Daily Advance*. "Even as a sheriff he was unpredictable."

Miller also disclosed that Currituck's ex-sheriff had suggested the county pay his legal bills.

"We have never paid legal bills before," Miller huffed. "I don't think we need to start here."

The article closed with an unnamed source mulling the possibility of a Brinkley/Johnson contest.

"If Glenn runs," that source conjectured, "it will be a good old Currituck County election—downright dirty."

In terms of power, in terms of clout, in Currituck County—perhaps everywhere—there is only one rival to land and that is influence, a.k.a. connections, a.k.a. generational networks.

See how they operate.

When I emailed the county's public information officer to confirm the dates of Glenn's employment, she conferred with Barbara Snowden née Blythe, who taught high school sociology to both the ex-sheriff and myself. Barbara Blythe Snowden lives across the street from the courthouse and is a member of the county historical society. The public information officer also forwarded my query to Currituck County's head librarian, also taught by Barbara Blythe Snowden in the same classroom that contained the future sheriff and myself. Quite possibly because the PIO failed to identify my past connection with the head librarian, my library-directed email went unanswered.

Last spring, Currituck County soil beneath my feet, I happened to mention to the wife of yet another cousin my frustrated hunt for Sheriff's Office info, whereupon she snapped: "Well, let's just get in the car and go on down there."

The destination "down there" no longer meant the cluster of historical buildings near the Knotts Island ferry dock where the Sheriff's Office had, for decades, been located. Soon after Glenn retired, those headquarters shifted to a prefab, buff-colored building on Maple Road, adjacent to what was once Maple Prison and is now the Maple Detention Center. The wife of my cousin stomped into the new but singularly unimpressive Sheriff's Office and I followed. Behind glass, a dressed-down receptionist and a stranger to us both (not an advantage) continued her phone chat. Many minutes passed. When finally the customer service face of the Sheriff's Office deigned to ask our business and I stated it, she reacted as if I had requested a comprehensive list of horse thieves living in the Dismal Swamp, circa 1790.

"Are you telling me the Sheriff's Office doesn't keep a file on the county's sheriffs?" demanded the wife of my cousin.

"I imagine somebody's got one somewhere," the receptionist replied, plainly not intending to pursue the whoever with access to the wherever, even if a taxpaying property owner spent the rest of the afternoon badgering her to do so.

When my mother heard about our failure at the Sheriff's Office, she took matters into her own hands.

"I'll call Sarah Ann." (Sister of ex-Sheriff Norman Jr.). "All those Newbern young'uns eat dinner at their mama's on Sunday. Sarah Ann can ask Norman Jr. then. He'll know."

True to prediction, Norman Jr. did know the service dates of both his predecessor and his successor, dates his sister copied down at her mama's dining room table, read to my mother over the phone and my mother, in turn, read to me.

Information transfer complete, kin to friend to kin.

Why had I bothered attempting to go through official channels? In Currituck County, going through official channels signals one of two inferiorities: either you're an outsider or you're a patsy. It also suggests you're not terribly invested in receiving a reply.

The Currituck Chamber of Commerce *Guide* celebrates "signs of development...everywhere, from the multi-family houses lining the beaches of the Currituck Outer Banks to...the just-completed middle school in Moyock." Seventy percent of the county's tax base is now derived from tourist dollars, and thus the "Currituck Chamber works hard to promote the area to new visitors" and to encourage "an aggressive development of the beaches."

—That last point presented as a Chamber of Commerce point of pride.

Not everyone in the county shares that sense of pride or views "aggressive development" as progress. At the fire stations and pool halls, at Ruritan Club and PTA meetings, at the grocery stores and gas pumps, few are shouting hallelujah over a public policy whose consequences are irreversible. Now and again you get the sense that a certain number of Currituck County residents wish their ancestors had never left the isolation of the Dismal Swamp.

Off Maple Road, offside the new sheriff's new digs, behind the renamed prison, is a small county-operated airport. Its single runway was recently extended by 1,500 feet—another Chamber of Commerce point of pride—the better to accommodate the arrival and departure of larger private aircraft. Rumor has it that the King of Jordan flew in a few months ago, deplaned, and travelled by limo to Blackwater U.S.A., a securities firm that has set up shop at the northern rim of the county, near Moyock. According to the company brochure, Blackwater offers "cost effective" anti-terrorism, firearms, "tactical driving" and "close-quarter battle" training to law enforcement agencies, multi-national corporations and "friendly nations around the globe." Among Blackwater's (named) clients: the U.S. Departments of Defense, State and Transportation. The Virginia Beach Police Department is also a Blackwater client—not so the Currituck County Sheriff's Department.

Anyone who calls ahead can sign up for a limited-scope tour of the Blackwater facilities, but stand on the edge of farmer Matt Wood's fields and gaze across the ditch bank and you're privy to pretty much all the limited-scope tour reveals. Target ranges, reconfigurable buildings, collapsible walls, ramming pads. Anyone who needs reminding of the new/old dichotomies still at play in a county Glenn Brinkley no longer patrols as sheriff should spend a moment in the weeds beside Matt Wood's field ditch. When that moment passes, the theorist/voyeur will itch from more than chigger bites.

Since my Blackwater tour ran shorter than anticipated, I had time to waste before my mother put supper on her table and expected her child there to eat it. And when I have time to myself back in the county of my birth, I like to spend it driving around, checking what's gone, what remains, what's been replaced, what's going up, what's been crowded out. Bells Island, off Route 168, is accessible by a road that floods every autumn and has flooded every autumn since the laying in of that access path. Once a single family's dairy farm, Bells Island is now an upscale community of homes large and larger, Glenn's among them.

I'm in a rental car, so who'd peg the driver for a native, someone who rode with the ex-sheriff's first posse?

Glenn lives now in a blue house with blue shutters on a cul-de-sac. His lot isn't quite waterfront property but affords a water view. There's a picket fence. There's a dog in the driveway. There's a swing set and an attached two-car garage. There's a *Virginian-Pilot* delivery box, one of the newspapers in whose pages Glenn's foibles were regularly exposed.

Big Earl is dead, Glenn's mama, Jean, also dead, of cancer. Glenn himself, scuttlebutt maintains, has completely recovered his health and vigor with no lingering side effects from his real/convenient heart attack. There's no reason the ex-sheriff can't relish his retirement, the love and companionship of his second wife and numerous offspring, thrive as a house husband and stay-at-home dad, drive his kids to school, call them in for supper and hear them say they'll be there in three or two minutes' time. No reason Glenn should spend a portion of each day for the rest of his lifetime thinking and rethinking about the October afternoon he slapped a troubled kid and what that slap set in motion.

But I suspect he does.

I suspect he gnaws at that bone day and night and night and day.

In the West

On Reading and Rereading *The Mind of the South* in No Place Southern

First impressions of author and book: a melancholic man, a melancholic text, the label in neither case a disparagement.

Southerners are a melancholic tribe.

I should have read W.J. Cash's classic years before I did. I owned the book, intended to read it but only opened my copy during a fit of melancholy retrospect ranks as minor. At the time, of course, the episode didn't feel minor. Blue moods seldom do.

During my first reading of *The Mind of the South*, I already counted as a South deserter. I finished 50 pages plunked on a splintered Adirondack chair that straddled gopher holes in a fenced backyard that smelled of orange blossoms. The house next door to my brown-shingled cottage in California still bore yellow tape from earthquake damage. Physically, I'd flown the Southern coop. Mentally? Not then, not now.

"If (the common Southerner) could not escape en masse, he could nevertheless escape as an individual…make (his) way out and on," Cash wrote and I read. In his leisure time, the Southerner "is free to brood as well as to dream—to exaggerate his fears as well as his hopes," Cash wrote and I read and brooded upon.

Next day, I came down with the flu, a defensible excuse for taking to bed. With me I took *The Mind of the South*, a decision that resulted in making the parts of me that didn't ache from a virus ache from other cause.

A sentimental reaction, Mr. Cash might call that—sentimentality a telltale Southern trait. He identified several others. Clannishness. The tendency to act and react with the "sensitiveness of a defeated people." A people of divided character: part hedonistic, part Puritanical. A people who carried individualism to violent extreme. Folks far too charmed by rhetoric and its flourishes. Romantics. Idealizers of the past. Unrealistic beings.

I can't argue with the list. Couldn't then. What I did do was insist that the reason I was weeping in bed in a brown-shingled cottage crumbling from dry rot was that I was *ill.* With the flu.

The flu is not insomnia nor insomnia the flu but both accommodate, not to say encourage, drifty thought. Last night, wide-eyed in my current bed, I drifted onto the topic of displacement(s). For a while I pondered the idea where I lay. Then, sleep an impossibility, I got up and headed for the living room where *displacement* merged with thoughts of *migration*, *migration patterns*, *Southern migration patterns*, *the migration patterns of Cracker farmers*, a series of associations that led me to search for my 12-year-old copy of *The Mind of the South* and, volume in hand, to reread Cash's gorgeous, melancholic descriptions of dirt workers who used and abused the soil before moving on.

My antecedents, those poor white farmers, those crass and craven, desperate men.

A blasphemous statement for a Southerner: someone, anyone, you don't know, have never met, related by blood or not, is just someone you don't know, have never met.

Blasphemy redux: the dead are only stories. If you remember at all, you remember the story.

Blood-kin Fritz would not only disagree with those two statements, she'd take furious offense. Self-appointed family historian, Sears side, Fritz labored long and hard on a project dear to her heart: researching our great-grandfather's Civil War records. Willoughby Dozier Barnard (1841-1914) served in Company B, 61st Virginia Infantry Regiment, 1861 to 1865. He was wounded twice, in the arm at Spotsylvania Court House and in the hip during the Siege of Petersburg. In April 1865 he was paroled as a prisoner of war at Appomattox Court House and headed home. Before and after the "great disaster of the Civil War and Reconstruction," in Cash's phrase, Willoughby Barnard was a piss poor farmer. On a good year, he cleared 50 bucks.

After Cousin Fritz completed her research, she compiled a booklet, Xeroxed it and sent copies to the full complement of Willoughby Barnard's descendants, including his 36 great-grandchildren, one in California. If ever I "made the time to come home," she wrote in a snide note attached, we ought to gather round Willoughby's field grave for a ceremony of remembrance.

I considered making the trip to stand over Willoughby's bones not for Willoughby's sake but to gaze upon Fritz as she reverently performed that homage. Because Fritz, unlike W.D. Barnard, is someone I actually know. Because we were kids together. Because when Fritz came down from Woodbridge, Virginia, to visit her North Carolina cousins, she came dressed "fancy," her mother's fashion style. Chiffon dresses, multi-tiered ruffles. Anklet socks edged with lace. In that outfit Fritz attempted to play in a farmyard of cows, cow pies, chickens, drooling curs, worms, fleas and sticky dirt. Which meant it was only a matter of time before Fritz in a white, sheer, ruffled dress stepped a white polished shoe into a cow pie and in her frantic attempt to escape cow shit lost her balance and fell into a ditch whose waters coursed below the outhouse.

"But let me take care not to exaggerate," Cash writes in *The Mind of the South*—a tempering I'd do well to emulate, describing Cousin Fritz.

When Cash died, purportedly he had started work on a novel described as a "novel of the South," the first of a proposed trilogy, spanning multiple generations. What might that first or second or third novel have read like? In *The Mind of the South*, Cash described both William Faulkner and Thomas Wolfe as writers who "hated the South with the exasperated hate of a lover who cannot persuade the object of his affections to his desire." He called the "Faulkners…the Caldwells…romantics of the appalling," then inquired: "Or am I mistaken in thinking that the essence of romanticism is the disposition to deal in the more-than-life-sized, the large and heroic, the picturesque and vivid and extravagant?"

The critic of rhetoric and romanticism falling sway to both.

Fundamental to romantic literature: the primacy of personal vision.

Self-inflicted death: a finale favored by romantics.

Born J.W. (Joseph Wilbur) Cash, the author reversed those initials and published as W.J. The son of South Carolinian Southern Baptists, he went north a state to Wake Forest College. He tried law school for a year, taught for a stretch, then settled into a journalism career. He wrote for the *Chicago Post,* H. L. Mencken's *American Mercury*, and the *Charlotte News*. The book *The Mind of the South* grew out of an article of the same title, published in the *Mercury*. Cash worked on the book manuscript for more than a decade while living with his parents in the North Carolina mountains. A large man, myopic, balding, he disliked public speaking. Doing so, his throat closed up on him. But along with fame came invitations to speak. And when invited to speak, he spoke.

In the space of a year, Cash's last, he published the book that made his reputation, married, won a Guggenheim grant, delivered the commencement address at the University of Texas, Austin, and ventured to Mexico where he died, July 1, 1941, at the age of 41, a celebrity author of five months, a half-year groom. In 1967, in the *Red Clay Reader*, his remarried widow published "The Suicide of W.J. Cash," her unromantic, unsentimental account of Cash's mind state in Mexico City and his death by necktie hanging in the couple's La Reforma Hotel room.

As the title suggests, Mary Cash Maury did not believe the Nazi spies Cash swore were tailing him in Mexico City served as his killers. She briefly describes their journey from North Carolina to Austin, the longer, more exhausting train ride "along the spine of Mexico." She mentions the Mexican heat, its disquieting effect on her husband.

Cash wrote this about Southern heat: "There are…days in July and August when the nerves wilt under the terrific impact of sun and humidity and even the soundest grow a bit neurotic."

Mexican heat makes Southern heat feel balmy.

Mary Cash Maury mentions intestinal distress, bouts of diarrhea, the fact that Cash was having trouble "accommodating his fingers to the small keyboard of the new portable typewriter he had bought in San Antonio." She mentions that her husband, when frustrated, bit his hands. She describes how he described the Nazi plot to kill them both and her subsequent attempts to "reason" with him. She recounts telephoning a fellow reporter, asking him to break the news of Cash's death to his parents. And then she describes the funeral, held in the First Baptist Church, Shelby, N.C., conducted by Cash's cousin. First the cousin apologized to God and the assembled for "cousin Wilbur's suicide." Then he apologized for Wilbur's "having maligned so many of (the) South's great men and institutions." Then he assured the crowd that, despite committing those most foul and insulting transgressions, Wilbur "had in reality been a very good boy."

Cousins.

Leave them behind, keep your distance, die, and still they get in their digs.

What I left, when I left the South, wasn't only depleted cropland—although I left plenty of that too. My desire to leave was inchoate but desire is always inchoate, a propellant as opposed to an explanation. As much homesick as flu-sick I was in that bed in that brown-shingled cottage. But homesick for what? Irrevocably gone by then: what I called "home," took for home, knew for home. As un-resurrectable as Willoughby Doxier Barnard. As lost as the cause he soldiered for.

"I have perhaps given the impression in passing," to borrow again from Cash, that I don't care about that loss, the distance between here and there, the gulf between now and then, the separation of me from mine. But that impression would be false. The hurt be what it feels, as my blood kin are apt to say. It be what it feels.

What Lies in Closets

It's long past two a.m. but not quite three. I'm roaming the house, listening to Leonard Cohen through headphones so as not to disturb the man and cat in residence who can sleep between two a.m. and three. Leonard Cohen's lugubrious lyrics, Leonard Cohen's dirge-like vocals: a soundtrack supremely suited to the walking exhausted.

More than halfway through my usual wandering circuit—kitchen/glass of water, living room/magazine rack, office/Internet connection—for no reason other than boredom, I deviate from routine, turn into a spare bedroom, yank open the closet door and begin to rifle through the boxes and bags of papers packed inside. There is stuff here I haven't touched since moving from my last address, files I haven't opened since moving East Coast to West.

Laying hands on a beat-about envelope marked *Patty Hearst,* listening to "Sisters of Mercy." A coincidence, yes. Also supremely apt. Although rumored to have been inspired by a three-way romp in a hotel room, Cohen's lyrics seek comfort from higher sources as well.

Comfort from sources high and low. Something Patricia Campbell Hearst, Catholic girl/heiress/victim/symbol could have used February 4, 1974, after dining on canned chicken noodle soup and tuna fish sandwiches in an apartment filled with macramé plant holders, after changing into a blue terrycloth robe to watch "Mission: Impossible" and "The Magician" on television, after trailing her fiancé to the door of 2603 Benvenue Avenue, Berkeley, at or around 9:20 p.m., when a female miming distress was so unwisely allowed to enter. Comfort gone missing during the beating of said fiancé and an abduction arc that included being dragged down steps, smacked in the face with a rifle butt, locked in a car trunk, tossed in the first "people's prison" in Daly City, site of her sleeping/unsleeping bed for (best estimate) 30 days prior to transfer to Golden Gate Avenue, San Francisco, for another (best estimate) 27 days of captivity inside closet number two. Comfort denied for 19 months in the company of eight, then two, who wished Death to the Fascist Insect that Preys on the Life of the People and on September 18, 1975, 2:25 p.m., when FBI agents raided 625 Morse Street, San Francisco, 592 days after the first apartment storming, and the fugitive they sought pissed her pants and surrendered without fight to another show of force. Comfort needed by a 90-pound "urban guerilla" continuously menstruating, en route to a collapsed lung and conviction for her part in the Hibernia Bank robbery, net proceeds $10,660, a prisoner who served 21 months of her seven-year sentence before President Jimmy Carter granted executive clemency and Prisoner 00077-181 walked out of the Federal Correctional Institution in Pleasanton with a flowered throw she'd crocheted, a guard dog named Arrow, a bodyguard boyfriend named Bernie, and, against all odds, a grin, her sanity and a sardonic sense of humor.

Comfort that was unjustly withheld—or not.

Depending on one's politics.

If, in the context of now, wearing my blue but not terrycloth bathrobe, I got in my car and drove without recklessness or excessive speed north on Interstate 880, I could be casing that Benvenue Avenue four-plex in an hour's time. If, instead of taking 880, I drove north on 280 into the city, in approximately the same travel time I could be rubbernecking the Morse Street capture site of Patty Hearst and apartment mate Wendy Yoshimura. Because now I reside in the Golden State's Bay Area.

In the context of then, February 1974, I lived weekdays in the Piedmont of North Carolina and on weekends drove 200+ miles east to overnight on my parents' farm. The purpose of that to and fro-ing was distraction. About what my personal future should contain, I could form no strong opinion. About what I *hoped* it would contain: equally fuzzy. The night the Symbionese Liberation Army kidnapped the heiress, a Monday night, I would have been back in the Piedmont, finished with another shift of my dead-end job and feeling grateful for the affections of a dog that considered me the center of his (limited) universe. Even so, I would have retained a parental-home-mindset because I needed until at least Tuesday evening each week to readjust to the idea that I was a grown, independent woman, living a life that supposedly confirmed those two adjectives. In effect I was someone who remained suspended between worlds, extremely susceptible to conditions of flux and float. As such, I was the ideal consumer of a story whose star exchanged one kind of existence for another without the bother of planning or input.

About Patty Hearst in 1974, I remember thinking: *She's not where she was. She's not by choice where she is. She's not free to return to what was, since altered. So what now?*

The file in my California closet contains the *Time* magazine issue with Patty/Tania's mug shot on the cover, part one of *Rolling Stone*'s account of Patty's cross-country escapades with the Harrises, and the ragged front page of the September 24, 1975 edition of the *Greensboro Daily News*, bearing these three headlines:

- Patty Swears Torture Drove Her to Insanity
- Mental Test Ordered for Sara Jane Moore
- "Squeaky" Ruled Competent to Stand Trial, Be Own Lawyer.

A slim file—but one that need not *remain* slim, I fast realize. Staring at the reproduced mug shot—the severely plucked brows, the limp and plastered hair, the dark and darker circles around those dim and vacant eyes—I sense I've stumbled on a bit of salvation. Even a minimal review of what has been written, filmed, argued and counter-argued about Patty Hearst since 1974 will take hours—many, many, many hours.

And so, as an insomniac, I think this about Patty Hearst: *goody*.

To quote Hannah Arendt: "Events, by definition, are occurrences that interrupt routine processes.... Predictions of the future are never anything but projections...of occurrences that are likely to come to pass if...nothing unexpected happens."

Nothing unexpected. Check.

To quote Patty turned Tania turned Patty Hearst, memoirist, in *Every Secret Thing*: "I...sense there is little one can do to prepare oneself adequately for the unknown."

Little one can do to prepare. Check.

To quote author/actress Patrica Hearst Shaw, speaking with Larry King in a broadcast that aired in 2002: "We all think we're pretty strong and that nobody can make us do something if we don't want to do it. That's true until somebody locks you up in a closet and tortures you and finally makes you so weak that you completely break."

True until. Check.

To quote John Wayne: "It seems quite odd to me that the American people have immediately accepted the fact that one man (Jim Jones) can brainwash 900 human beings into mass suicide (in Guyana), but will not accept the fact that a ruthless group, the Symbionese Liberation Army, could brainwash a little girl by torture, degradation and confinement."

Torture, degradation, confinement. Check. (And note that "little girl.")

A self-styled revolutionary corps of ten, the SLA's membership roster contained two in jail for the murder of Oakland Superintendent of Schools

Marcus Foster, a preponderance of females and a preponderance of college-educated ex-suburbanites. Acting under the leadership of the SLA's single black member, General Field Marshall Cinque (a.k.a. Donald DeFreeze), the group decides to snatch a UC Berkeley undergrad, a 19-year-old rich bitch from Hillsborough slumming it with her grad-school boyfriend on Benvenue Avenue.

Rather remarkably, their scheme succeeds.

I first read Shana Alexander's *Anyone's Daughter: The Times and Trials of Patty Hearst* when it was published in 1979. Second time through, what's most striking is how very much Alexander dislikes Catherine Hearst, that "brightly Lana Turnerish," yet also "strangely Chinese" woman with "tiny feet," "cotton-candy hair," and "flawless makeup."

About Mrs. Hearst's mental makeup, Ms. Alexander reports: "A special kind of perfection also marks this woman's mind. It is not a perfection of stupidity, though her singlemindedness can make her appear that way."

About Mrs. Hearst's environment, the Hillsborough community, Ms. Alexander reports: "Hillsborough does not produce people with flexible minds…without doubt the most boring enclave of privilege I had ever visited, lacking weather or even scenery to fall back on when in conversational distress."

About the interview with Mrs. Hearst that appeared in the July 1974 *Ladies Home Journal*, Ms. Alexander reports: "The article is heavy on Catherine's hobbies—stargazing, supermarketing, and the study of the genealogy of the ancient royal family of Hawaii."

About Catherine Hearst's background, Ms. Alexander reports: "In the late 1930s…Catherine Campbell, the belle of Atlanta, was a finalist in the nation-wide Scarlett O'Hara contest to find an unknown actress to star opposite Clark Gable in *Gone with the Wind*…. Catherine Campbell Hearst is, before everything, a Southern girl. She would no more reveal her true feelings in public than she would sit with her legs uncrossed."

That "Southern girl" remark.

Southern born, I am particularly (perhaps too particularly) alert to Southern bashing. A hundred pages or so into *Anyone's Daughter*, I begin to suspect the Southern slur trumps the Hillsborough slur in Ms. Alexander's ranking of insults. I begin to suspect Ms. Alexander went looking for a weeping, wailing mother in visible distress, hair uncombed, dress askew, and when she found instead a steely Southerner determined never to let the "public" see her "crack," I suspect the contradiction pissed off Ms. Alexander. I suspect that development threatened the narrative already scrolling inside Ms. Alexander's head if not yet transferred onto the page.

Also not a Catherine fan: Steven Weed, once prospective son-in-law. Weed pans Mrs. Hearst's "insular upbringing," "overreliance on prescribed drugs," and lack of mothering skills. Her fervent Catholicism, he asserts in *My Search for Patty Hearst*, "only increased her inability to come to grips with an increasingly secular world. Though a member of the Board of Regents, no one could have been less well suited to...understand the problems at Berkeley."

Mid-trial, Patty's lawyer, F. Lee Bailey, describes Catherine Hearst as a "terrible pessimist. Deep down she thinks that...her daughter will go to jail."

A jab on Bailey's part.

However: her daughter did indeed go to jail. Which means Catherine Hearst called it exactly right. Which means Mrs. Hearst was in actuality less a terrible pessimist than a gritty realist.

According to both Alexander and Weed, Catherine Hearst castigates her daughter's fiancé for falling short of the Clark Gable/Rhett Butler manliness bar. "Whatever happened to the real men in this world?" she hisses at Weed. "Men like Clark Gable. No one would have carried off my daughter if there had been a real man there!"

When Steven Weed meets Catherine Hearst's daughter at the Crystal Springs School for Girls, he's 23, Patty's teacher. She's 17. In *My Search for Patty Hearst*, Weed insists Patty pursued him, not vice versa. If so, he's an easy catch. Promptly he dumps the woman he's then living with for the heiress. His "tiny, small-boned and compact, almost childlike" new lover—a merely "competent cook"—has a "choppy, determined little step" and is "never one to suffer a lack of confidence." In her daddy-bought MG, they zoom off to vacations at the Hearst family retreats, San Simeon to the south, Wyntoon to the north. They get engaged. They plan to marry because Patty wants to get married—not because Weed sees an opportunity to live off a trust fund. (Perish the thought.)

In Patty's counter-version of that place and time, she complains: "Most of our friends at Berkeley were *his* friends...." When those friends visit, her fiancé discourses "for hours on some minute point of nineteenth-century philosophy or English punctuation." Bored, she "slip(s) away to the kitchen" to bake a cake. "I came to see that my first true love was not perfect," she writes. "He was not only intelligent and self-confident; he was also arrogant and condescending." As the wedding date approaches, the pending bride experiences "doubts and fears." To escape the nuptials, she considers "joining the Navy." She also slides into a "depression." Others assure her pre-wedding jitters are quite normal. She tries to believe that bromide—but does she?

February fourth.

The pending groom of a willing/unwilling bride passes another day studying philosophy, another (half) night in front of the television. Then comes the fateful knock on the door. Attacked, battered and bleeding, Weed escapes the apartment, runs out the rear door and onto the patio, leaps over a fence, then over a second fence before realizing, in his own words, "no one was chasing me"—those no ones otherwise preoccupied with dragging his fiancée down the steps and stashing her inside the trunk of their getaway car.

Running in the opposite direction.

Not what Catherine Hearst would classify as a real-man response.

Steven Weed, the fellow Patty never again sees or speaks to after the kidnapping, publishes his book six years before she publishes hers. He "turned to writing because it was therapeutic," he informs Shana Alexander, and part of that therapy seems to be listing further screw-ups and/or embarrassments. Called into U.S. District Attorney James Browning's office to identify one of the Hibernia Bank robbers, he tells Browning "of course" it's Patty, signs the back of the photograph as evidence of that identification, agrees to "appear before the grand jury as a character witness" and only "halfway down the stairs" realizes he's just helped "build the case" against his former roommate. Dining with an "attractive young reporter" from *Newsday*, he gets "pleasantly high" and supplies a "tape recorder full of raw material" that results in an article that both infuriates and dumbfounds the usually genial Randolph Hearst. "What the hell is with you? You get up there with some girl...and just bubble like a yeastcake."

Toward the end of *My Search for Patty Hearst*, Weed declares his "disappointment" with Patty and states that when he thinks of her as a "victim," he still loves her, but when he thinks she's acting in the manner of a "spoiled brat," he loves her not.

Getting kidnapped is a high price to pay for getting shed of Steven Weed, but too high?

Debatable.

Arrogance. Presumption. Cockiness.

In 1974, many younger than 30 in America assumed the divine right to pronounce and denounce. If we disagreed with governmental policy, we expected that government to listen. If we were against a war, we expected its prompt end. If we disliked the "leader of the free world," we expected him and entourage to pack bags for exile in San Clemente. If we rejected monogamy, materialism, the house/car/kids model of achievement, we expected our dissension to be more than tolerated. We expected loud applause. Accordingly, if we fancied someone, we insisted that someone could and should be ours for a night or long weekend sans regrets, recriminations, or the mess and muck of further entanglement.

In retrospect, what seems most striking about that era's sense of entitlement was its nonexclusive, democratic base. A certain segment of the young in any era assume entitlement because their heritage and daily circumstance support the snobbery. But in the late sixties and early seventies, scholarship students, farm children, the offspring factory wages fed and clothed, also believed and behaved as if we too counted among the anointed. Backed by several generations of wealth, Patty Hearst qualified as old-school privileged. Her age and college of choice made her one of the new-school privileged as well. It was a risk: combining an old-school bank account with new-school accessibility, and it got her kidnapped.

Privilege, entitlement—neither concept holds up well under adverse circumstances. Fifty-seven days of closet confinement, for example.

The first closet in Daly City: 5 1/2 feet long, 2 feet deep.

The second closet on Golden Gate Avenue: 5 feet long, 1 foot 7 inches deep.

My 600-square-foot 1974 rental off the Chapel Hill/Durham bypass featured a 5'x2' bedroom closet. The enclosure barely accommodated the width of a coat hanger. Sticking an arm inside to snatch a blouse incited my claustrophobia. Her tiny compactness aside—height 5'2" or 5'3", depending on the source, weight 110 pounds going in—Patty Hearst survived inside those people's prisons cramped and crimped, sleep-, light-, and fresh-air deprived. It is beyond my capacity to imagine confinement in such close quarters 57 days and nights.

The kidnapped says she was transferred in a plastic garbage can from the closet of the Daly City safe house to the closet on Golden Gate Avenue. Not surprisingly, Bill and Emily Harris say otherwise. They say the abducted was never confined to any closet; that the door of the Daly City closet was always open; that her hands were never tied. They also say Patty Hearst spent no time whatsoever in the Golden Gate Avenue closet because by then she was a certified SLAer renamed Tania.

Much of *Every Secret Thing* reads like a forced, if precise, recitation of what happened when, but not the descriptions of closet confinement and its effects. Those lift the neck hairs. Blindfolded, she's tossed inside. She's bleeding on the leg, her face still throbs from the earlier rifle butt blow. Her tears soak through the blindfold, lubricating it, causing it to slip. She's terrified she'll be blamed for that readjustment and terror makes her cry harder. The closet stinks of "sweat and filth." As crude soundproofing, old carpet remnants have been nailed to the walls and door, ceiling to floor. "I might as well have been in an underground coffin," she writes. Time passes, but how much? She can't distinguish night from day. Maybe she sleeps, maybe she doesn't. Above all else, she feels "uncontrollable fear" of being killed by captors whom she "could not stop" from killing her.

During Hearst's closeting, she loses 15 pounds of fighting weight and comes to despise (among other things) the smell and taste of peppermint tea. When allowed out of the closet to pee, she does so blindfolded, with an audience. Her first bath: also with blindfold intact, also with an audience. She asks if she can remove the blindfold to wash her hair and face, bath two. "They held a meeting on that," she writes, a bit of sarcasm that quickly vanishes, even in recall. "I was so thankful for that bath and hair wash one would have thought I was being led to a party…." In the bathroom, when the blindfold comes off: "Everything looked so strange, so out of proportion. Everything around me appeared huge, distorted and constantly moving like ocean waves."

Back in the closet, she wakes from a "fitful" nap, convinced she's dying. She realizes that even if she were "free to walk away," she can't because she can't stand without assistance. "I was so tired, so tired; all I wanted to do was to sleep…and I knew that was…fatal, like the man lost in the Arctic snow, who, having laid his head down for that delicious nap, never woke again."

Afraid to sleep.

In my universe, that comment scans like punishment reserved for hell.

In the 1988 film *Patty Hearst*, directed by Paul Schrader and based on *Every Secret Thing*, the protagonist is played by Natasha Richardson, daughter of Vanessa Redgrave, a fairly radical lass herself. For much of the film, the camera's view is the closet view: the darkness and shadow, the visual and audial skew, the activity outside it, the terror within. Limited set, small cast, a film with the look and feel of a play, Richardson's voiceover narration a pitch perfect rendition of her character's speech—a monotonic flatness that rises, almost imperceptibly, when delivering a sting.

No hint of sarcasm in the first communiqué, recorded in the closet. Neither on the actual tape, as included in Robert Stone's documentary *Guerrilla: The Taking of Patty Hearst*, nor on the tape's filmic recreation, delivered by mimic Richardson.

"Mom" (pause) "Dad" (pause) "I'm" (pause) "okay" (pause).

When Hearst records that tape she's not okay or anything close to that state of being but she's still breathing. A victory of sorts. Another unchartable chunk of time passes. She's still in the closet. And it's inside that closet that she resolves not to die "of (her) own accord," to "concentrate on staying alive one day at a time."

Once she stops fearing second by second for her life, once fear transforms into something like adrenaline jolts caused by a voice, a movement, a second uninvited body joining her in that closet, I have no trouble believing Patty Hearst resolves to play the odds. No trouble believing that she finds it inconceivable that Hearst money, influence and power haven't yet set her free. Even less trouble believing that after swinging a gun in a bank lobby and joining the ranks of the FBI's Most Wanted and crisscrossing the country and *still* not being found by any of those supposedly looking so hard and desperately for her, she concludes this: whatever life has become is probably the way life is going to stay. Deal or die. The burning question being: did she deal by converting or by conning?

"Liberated" from the closet, her first opportunity to match faces with voices, I like to think the granddaughter of gamesman William Randolph Hearst masterminds a gullibility test. When the blindfold comes off and she utters that ludicrous but very well played "You're all so attractive" remark, I like to think W.R.'s granddaughter does so for reasons other than terror and despair. If the SLA "militia" growls and grumbles and reminds her that "attractiveness" is hardly a deciding factor in the violent overthrow of the American government, the response confirms opponents of a certain cast. If, on the other hand, they grin like vainglorious fools, as they do in the Schrader film, there's wiggle room.

Enter Tania, stage left.

Attractiveness.

Sexual desire, after 57 days and nights in a closet.

Even in a contentious trial, the prosecution doesn't dispute defense testimony that sexual feelings are among the first to go for persons held captive, a psychological/physiological finding relevant to the pairing off of Patty/Tania and Willie/Cujo, a prep school grad, a UC Berkeley undergrad whose interest in prison reform leads him to Black Cultural Association meetings at Vacaville Prison and into the orbit of Donald DeFreeze, a doctor's son who renounces college to be a grunt in General Field Marshal Cinque's army. At

23, Willie Wolfe, the youngest captor, is closest in age and background to the captive.

At her trial, Hearst swears she couldn't "stand" the guy. Regardless, fictioneers (Christopher Sorrentino in *Trance* and others) prefer guerilla love to rape and revulsion. In the final communiqué, Hearst calls Willie/Cujo the "gentlest, most beautiful man" she's "ever known" and declares neither of them "ever loved an individual the way we loved each other." She sports his Olmec monkey gift around her neck until the Los Angeles inferno and thereafter keeps it in her purse, where it's found by the FBI. The fact that she saved that gewgaw? Also a gift to the prosecution. She *must* have loved the slain. But what if, upon release from closet number two, still shaky in the legs and unsure of her ability to escape entire, W.R.'s granddaughter sizes up her partnering options and deems Willie Wolfe the lesser evil? What if she displays the trinket around her neck only as long as the giver is around to expect/demand that show of devotion and afterward hedges her bets by stashing the trinket in her purse?

It's a theory.

During the trial, the prosecution refers to Patty Hearst's "unparalleled capacity for sarcasm." Hyperbole, one hopes, given the sarcasm fodder daily provided by the SLA. The plum wine cache. The combat drills in the hallways of safe houses. The sexual politics of who would sleep with the General and who with the hierarchy's lesser lights. Angela Atwood, Nancy Ling Perry, Patricia Soltysik and latter day SLA convert Kathy Soliah—all actress wannabes, according to former San Francisco *Chronicle* reporter Tim Findley. Picture it: the granddaughter of the paramour of Marion Davies competing for the role of most convincing urban guerilla, an actress-in-training long before she meets John Waters.

First stage credit: the role of Tania.

First film appearance: the Hibernia Bank Robbery.

Costume: shag wig and trench coat.

Prop: semi-automatic carbine.

Because she's so convincing in the role of bank robber/terrorist, her comrades assure her she'll now most definitely be shot if captured/recaptured. Welcome to the club, comrade. If Patty/Tania initially doubts the dire prediction, what occurs in L.A. must look a lot like confirmation.

Because Bill Harris/Teko can't refrain from shoplifting a pair of socks (a bandolier, he claims) from Mel's Sporting Goods on May 16, because in the scuffle he loses a Colt revolver registered in the name of Emily Harris, because Emily/Yolanda insists they abandon Cinque's VW van, the police discover the safe house on West 84th Street and then the very un-safe safe house on East 54th Street. From a Disneyland motel room, May 17, Patty/Tania and the Harrises watch the firefight and barbeque that ends the lives of six SLA grandees, including General Field Marshal Cinque who, according to autopsy reports, doesn't quite go down with the ship or in like fashion with his comrades, but dies of a self-inflicted bullet to the brain à la Hitler.

Interviewed by Larry King almost 30 years later, Patty Hearst is once again pressed to explain "how she felt" about the shootout.

KING: Now, you've been kidnapped for 90 days when this famous shootout occurred. Where were you?

HEARST: I'm trying to think now. In a motel with the Harrises.

KING: Were you watching this?

HEARST: Yes.

KING: What did you think?

HEARST: Of…? You know, they were saying the whole time that they thought that I was in there."

In there, dying, with the rest.

Does or doesn't the FBI and the Los Angeles Police Department believe she's inside that East 54th Street bungalow? Patty/Tania assumes they do, and still the bullets fly and the fire burns.

In the SLA's arsenal: four automatic weapons, six shotguns, six handguns and various pipe bomb materials. The LAPD's counterforce: 9,000 bullets, 125 tear-gas canisters, 321 police vehicles, 2 helicopters, 410 siege officers, and 196 crowd-control and security officers. Not counting the FBI surcharge, Shana Alexander estimates eradicating six SLA members cost the government approximately $68,000.

And Patty/Tania's fate once that directive is accomplished? To flee fire, death and L.A. via Interstate 5, that speedway renowned for multi-car collisions, tipped big rigs, fog-outs, dust storms, and a Denny's restaurant every two exits. To embark on another feckless chapter of life on the lam hidden beneath a blanket in the backseat of a car that also contains the least winsome pair of a not very winsome lot: Teko and Yolanda.

Teko and Yolanda/Bill and Emily Harris.

A strain on the nerves in the best of circumstances.

He's volatile, a ranter, a hitter, the shortest guy on the playground, the white guy who desperately wants to be black. Her manipulations are more covert and cunning, a schoolmarm in revolutionary garb. She's overly fond of discipline, of punishing slackers who fall short. As a twosome they bicker incessantly, neurotically enmeshed but determined to behave as if they have thrown off the bourgeois pox of manners and monogamy.

Willie Wolfe she "couldn't stand," but Hearst's reaction to the Harrises is far more scathing and intense. That "violent, evil, unpredictable, incompetent" pair she "loathed," and Wendy Yoshimura, who joins the entourage on the East Coast, seems to share Hearst's low opinion of the two. Unlike the Harrises, during the summer of farm hideouts, Yoshimura comports herself with calm discretion, a model of levelheaded reliability. Back in the Bay Area, Yoshimura and Patty/Tania set up house apart from the Teko/Yolanda sideshow. No doubt a welcome respite. Also extremely short lived. The Tania part of the Patty story is all but done.

September 5, 1975. Sacramento. Lynette "Squeaky" Fromme attempts to kill President Gerald Ford with a .45 caliber Colt.

September 18, 1975. San Francisco. Fugitive Patty/Tania is captured in an apartment with two communal carbines and her own personal revolver.

September 22, 1975. San Francisco. Sara Jane Moore attempts to kill President Gerald Ford with a .38 caliber Smith & Wesson.

Violent femmes.

Guerrilla girls.

Girls and guns.

In California, an outbreak, a convergence, of girls and guns.

Newly jailed, Patty/Tania can't remember the courses she took at Berkeley or where her sisters went to school. Her scores on the Minnesota Multiphasic Personality Inventory place her in the "feebleminded" range. After 19 months with the SLA and its remnants, Patty Hearst takes the Sentence Completion Test, whose diagnostic purpose is to provide "insights into the defenses, fears and preoccupations of the patient," and finishes these starters thus:

My greatest trouble is the present and the past, and I guess the future too.

The dark it's there, I mean.

Death you have to accept it.

In the opinion of *Guerilla* documentarian Robert Stone, Patty Hearst should have been treated as "an ordinary young woman who got kidnapped and joined a cult." In the taped communiqués that range in sentiment from *Mom, Dad, I'm okay* to *I hope I can get back really soon* to ditch the black dress,

Mom, I'm not dead to *I don't think you're doing everything you could do, Dad* to *I've decided to stay and fight* to proclaimed adoration for that most beautiful of men, the dead Cujo, Stone says, "You can feel her transforming her personality. That's what happens in cults."

Instead of advising his client to throw herself on the mercy of the court, F. Lee Bailey and team opt to argue brainwashing.

When the jury files in to deliver the verdict, according to Shana Alexander, before that verdict is announced, Patty Hearst mouths the word "guilty," suggesting that over the course of an abduction, closet captivity, life on the run, San Mateo County jail incarceration and trial preparation, the defendant has become marvelously adept at reading the expressions, intuiting the decisions and anticipating the actions of those in whose hands her fate depends.

"I don't blame them," Patty Hearst says of the jury who convicts her. "Unless they had been there, there was no way they could understand."

No way.

Details of the sort that stick:

Emily Harris appropriating the blue terrycloth robe Hearst was wearing when abducted, laundering it, repairing the tears and curling up in that garment across the room from its previous owner.

Patty/Tania sharing "pig lookout" duty with Cinque her first night out of the closet, the two of them staring through razor slits in the curtains, 11 p.m. to 2 a.m.

The People In Need/Hearst food giveaway administrator cum FBI informer cum would-be assassin Sara Jane Moore who, asked how to report the hijacking of a Hearst-supplied food truck, quips: "Start it with, 'Once upon a time there was a truck.'"

A Download-for-Free! essay on essayexpress.com whose cadence, concept, reasoning and punctuation are the stuff of teacher nightmare. "She lived in a mansion...she was a woman who was part of some crimes."

A mansion-dweller, a perpetrator of "some crimes."

Patty Hearst, Trivial Pursuit category.

At the end of the movie *Patty Hearst*, Richardson as Hearst remarks in trademark deadpan fashion: "I finally figured out what my crime was. I lived."

Lived through what to become what?

Body snatch, closet confinement, SLA menace and braggadocio, the perpetual fear of being killed by comrade or G-man. Capture and transport to another lock in/lock up, this one with actual bars, where dead rats appear on her mattress and her menses won't stop and her lung collapses and those who supposedly love her won't fire the showboat lawyer who advises her to take the fifth 42 times on the witness stand. A conviction, a jail term that brings her to the letter-writing attentions of correspondent Charlie Manson and ultimately to the attention of President Jimmy Carter who issues—after almost two years of time served—an order of executive clemency.

The publication of a tell-all memoir that begins with a list of her civilian-life protections (locked doors, home security systems, additional guard dogs, firearms). Marriage, two months out of prison, to her bodyguard, a man who looks to make about three of Steven Weed. Glammed up, fattened up, this Patty Hearst incarnation promotes her book on talk shows, explains what she will ever after have to explain, justify and defend: what she did, why and when at the ages of 19 and 20. She hosts a televised tour of San Simeon for the Travel Channel. She coauthors a mystery slash historical romance set at San Simeon featuring passages of dialog and passions a-tumble such as: "'Lucas,' she repeated, while he slid to the couch and wrapped her up in his strong, sure arms."

Not just arms: strong, sure, Rhett Butler-esque arms.

She becomes a fixture on the East Coast/New York social scene, organizes charity events, poses arm-in-arm with her two daughters, one a Paris Hilton doppelgänger. She co-stars in films by John Waters, once playing the mother of a kidnapping terrorist. On his way out of Dodge, President Bill Clinton grants her a presidential pardon.

She celebrates—or ignores—her fifty-first birthday. Her mother is dead. Her father is dead. Along with several cousins, she sues the Hearst Family Trust for access to financial records sealed to thwart the ransom demands of SLA copycats. Heading toward another courtroom, impeccably groomed (her mother would be so proud), she is run at and jostled by reporters on deadline. Microphones and cameras thrust in her face, her eyes go a little opaque but she responds to the shouted questions, gives the newshounds a quote ("It's a free speech issue") and walks on, walks on.

In the house she lives in there are closets—there must be. Closets more capacious, it's fair to guess, than the closets of her imprisonment, but closets all the same with doors that shut and possibly lock. On occasion, Patricia Hearst Shaw, wife, mother, matron, must have cause to step into one or another of her closets and be reminded of closet parameters and the darkness that collects inside once closet doors are closed.

Patricia Hearst Shaw sleeps in a house with closets.

Stunning, isn't it?

Craters in the Sand
(Why No One Should Sleep Easy)

The Atomic Testing Museum, at 755 East Flamingo Road, sits mere blocks from Las Vegas Boulevard, home to the mega casinos. To depart, as I did, Steve Wynn's Italianate Bellagio and arrive at the Atomic Testing Museum is to exchange one surreality for another—surreal being the operating system in play this warm June day. The extent to which the actual, the observable and the documented will, over the course of the next eight hours, run up hard against the scarcely imaginable hasn't yet been realized by those of us signed up for the once-monthly public tour of the Nevada Test Site, formerly the Nevada Proving Ground, a chunk of desert roughly the size of Rhode Island, 65 miles west/northwest of the city, site of 928 atmospheric and underground nuclear tests, because, for the moment, we're just getting started.

Absolutely prohibited: shorts, skirts, sandals, cameras, tape recorders, cell phones, binoculars, firearms, anyone under the age of 14 (with or without a parent). Absolutely required: photo ID, valid passport or alien registration card. Bring your own lunch. No meal provided.

It's 6:45 a.m., 70-something degrees in the non-shade. Balmy for Vegas, though fast leaving that comfort zone. Squinting is a given with or without sunglasses. Despite the hour, many are out and about, early risers mixed in with the never-to-beds. Traffic is brisk, thick and screechy, already a game of dash and swerve.

I, myself, have been awake since three, dressed since four, coffee-ed up since five. Since 6:15, I've been parked in the Atomic Testing Museum parking lot and even so don't count as first on the scene. Two arrived before me. One fellow is wearing the verboten shorts; another is catching a few winks in his sand-blasted, sun-baked car, its back windshield soaped with a question: "Where's the compassion?" On the basis of the shorts wearer and compassion seeker, I initially assume ours will be something of a "protest" tour—but no. As it happens, once we reach our full complement, we're a fairly diverse group. College students, senior citizens, life-long civilians, military vets, Americans, Europeans, rabid conspiracists and rabid patriots, all of us along for the ride.

Once inside the museum, we're encouraged to shop the gift store. In addition to books about the Test Site, the Cold War and non-national defense uses of nuclear power, there are caps, mugs, t-shirts, Miss Atomic Bomb 1957 refrigerator magnets and mushroom cloud computer mouse pads. Free for the taking: U.S. Department of Energy post-it notes that appear to include, as background, an irradiated Joshua tree.

Although I don't generally consider myself the superstitious sort, I'm less than thrilled that my ID badge for the tour pairs a synonym for transience with a bad luck numeral: Temp 113. We are told by the Atomic Testing Museum librarian that we must "*always* display our badges above waist level"—instructions blatantly ignored by several who clip their badges to their shirttails and leave them just so.

Perhaps because I already have my notebook out, an elderly but spry man wearing a baseball cap and glasses thicker than mine sidles over. Without introducing himself, he leans in to confide, sotto voce, that the "Yucca people" have a "contract" on his "head." He is referring to the controversial Yucca Mountain Project and proposed repository for radioactive waste located within the Nevada Test Site boundaries—I'm clear on that—but until the librarian comes by to insist Jacob Paz visibly display his ID badge, I don't know the confider's name. Once I do know, I'm able to fill in a few gaps because Dr. Jacob Paz's reputation precedes him. A scientist and former Test Site employee, he has a habit of turning up at public meetings of the Environmental Protection Agency and Nuclear Waste Technical Review Board to point out "flaws in the risk assessment" standards of the Yucca Mountain Project, express his concern about radionuclide issues, and very probably undermine the force of his arguments by requesting research funds to validate his objections.

Why is Dr. Jacob Paz taking the public tour of his former workplace?

Curious.

Roger, the tour guide assigned to the second bus, my bus, is a 79-year-old retired radiation physicist who worked at the Test Site for 32 years and received, shortly after his hiring, "one fifth of his lifetime radiation" from the 1962 Sedan detonation. He reports the statistic in jocular, upbeat fashion. With few exceptions, throughout the day, Roger's mode of information delivery about subjects specific, general, personal and abstruse will remain slaphappily upbeat—disconcertingly so. When he isn't answering questions or popping in a video for us to watch between tour stops, he often whistles. Once I believe I recognize the theme song to the "Big Valley" TV show, but my seatmate insists it's the theme song to "Dallas."

On the road, but still within Vegas city limits, Roger takes up the microphone to tell us we'll observe "everything that can be shown" at the Test Site and promises he'll answer as many questions as possible. For security reasons, there are certain questions he can't and won't answer, under threat of a "$10,000 fine and 10 years in prison." Then he provides a quick and streamlined overview of the Test Site's operational history. Prior to the 1992 worldwide moratorium on nuclear testing, there were two distinct testing "eras": the atmospheric era (1951-1958) and the underground era (1961-1992). Test types included air drops, tower drops, surface, balloon, shaft and tunnel detonations. Not every blast tested weapon capacity. Some measured weapon effects and others weapon "safety." When the Russians resumed testing in 1961 in open defiance of the 1958 U.S./Russia moratorium agreement, the United States responded by conducting, in 1962, 96 nuclear detonations at NTS, the highest number carried out in a single year before that date and (thus far) since.

Someone from the back of the bus asks how many people work at the Test Site. The current number of employees, Roger doesn't know, but, back in the 1960s, "as many as ten thousand" were on the payroll. Someone closer, who doesn't have to shout her question to catch Roger's attention, asks whether we'll be touring the Climax Facility, a spent-fuel test facility located in Area 15. Definitely not, Roger says. Even apart from security issues, an all-inclusive tour isn't feasible. Getting to the Test Site in Nye County is a 65-mile trip, one-way; the Test Site itself covers 1,350 square miles of desert and mountain terrain. He reminds us that we are enjoying a free tour (which, remarkably, it is, although some portion of our tax dollars must be going to pay for the USA coach and driver) and assures us that at no point during the tour will we be exposed to toxic levels of radiation. During the day, he hopes to "set straight a few misunderstandings" but promises to refrain from "out and out propagandizing."

A scientist turned promoter is Roger.

There's a lot of that going around.

Yesterday, inside the Atomic Testing Museum, I saw Troy Wade, former Assistant Secretary of Energy for Defense Programs, U.S. Department of Energy, ushering a party of three exhibit to exhibit. I recognized Mr. Wade because he appears in numerous NTS videos describing his former duties as Test Site director, project manager and detonation countdown man. These days, as chair of the NTS Historical Foundation, he's responsible for fundraising and for organizing donor galas such as the sunset cruise on Lake Las Vegas that celebrated the museum's opening.

Troy Wade.

A nuclear weapons expert reduced to glad-handing.

The museum, an affiliate of the Smithsonian, is (perhaps intentionally) claustrophobic and bunker-like: winding hallways, dark walls, low ceilings. In the Ground Zero Theatre, visitors are treated to a simulated ground zero/ atmospheric detonation experience: a bright, bright flash of light, black skies turned white, a rush of heat, billowing fire and smoke and sand and debris, a shock wave boom, ground heaving beneath one's feet, the birth and ascension of a purple, pink and orange mushroom cloud.

A simulation only.

Even so, profoundly unnerving.

There's a photograph of Jack Kennedy visiting the Test Site in 1962, that test-high year, a standout among the khaki wearers in his dark suit and dark glasses. He is President of the United States, Commander in Chief, Leader of the Free World, but in that photo, in that photo's context, he looks remarkably like a Vegas celebrity. Another oversized photo, first published in a 1952 issue of *Collier's* magazine, shows kids in front of Vegas tract houses. In the photo, alongside white picket fences, they have assumed "the position," lying face down in sand, bicycles tossed aside, a mushroom cloud adrift in the sky. One of the girls has curled her arm around the shoulder of another, as if to protect. It's just a test. The kids in that picture are alive. They just don't appear to be.

Also on display: a two-page newspaper ad, paid for by JC Penney, featuring mannequins attired in JC Penney-wear. The ad is laid out in the manner of a high school yearbook. Row after row of mannequins, dressed to impress, on the verge of embracing their destiny (mutilation by detonation). It could so easily be someone's idea of a perverse joke. But it isn't. It isn't.

There is a video showing the annihilation of a "Colonial home," built 3,500 feet from 16-kiloton Annie's ground zero. An atmospheric tower drop and the first nationally televised nuclear shot, Annie took place on March 17, 1953 and completely destroyed the demo home in fewer than three seconds. The Annie video at the museum is interactive. It can be run backward, forward, or stopped at any point. Destroy, reassemble, freeze frame. Visitor's choice. You control the knobs.

The last exhibit in the museum combines a chunk of Berlin Wall with a chunk of the World Trade Center. Yesterday, standing in front of those artifacts, Troy Wade told his companions: "The war hasn't ended. It's just a different kind of war." Pleased as I was to record that overheard remark, I needn't have bothered. The phrase turns out to be something of a Troy Wade standard, printed, reprinted, broadcast and rebroadcast in Vegas and elsewhere.

From the get-go, the movers and shakers of Vegas, as well as the hoi polloi, welcomed all things atomic. The Clark County official seal of the 1950s incorporated a mushroom cloud. Every Miss Atom Bomb, in her off hours, performed as a Vegas showgirl. The casinos served up "atomic cocktails," bubbly, tooth-tingling, gut-churning mixtures of vodka, brandy, champagne and sherry. On test days, natives and tourists rose before dawn to line the roadways, climb onto rooftops and settle on lawn chairs to witness the sound and light show. Tests in the Ranger series shattered windows in downtown Vegas. North winds blew Baker Two's mushroom cloud off course, producing radioactive snow on the far side of the country. In 1953, Harry (a.k.a. Dirty Harry), a 32-kiloton tower drop, sent the "downwinder" residents of St. George, Utah, indoors for two hours. In 1956, there was an "unplanned' 4-kiloton blast. In 1970, during the "Baneberry venting," in a "spectacular release" of radioactivity, a plume of gas and dust 10,000 feet high drifted and spewed, spewed and drifted.

But the band(s) played on.

Once we reach Highway 95, Roger pops in a video and tells the bus driver to "wake him when we get there"—a reference to the Mercury exit, apparently.

Refreshed by his nap, Roger animatedly calls our attention to the two chain-link fences surrounding porta potties to our immediate left, just shy of the Test Site entry gate.

Holding pens for protestors, Roger informs.

"Martin Sheen, the TV president? He's been in there *many* times."

Two contractors currently manage the Test Site: the Nevada division of Bechtel Corporation, the corporation overseeing the U.S.'s Infrastructure Reconstruction Program in Iraq, and Wackenhut, a securities firm. At the gate, a very young Wackenhut guard boards the bus to announce what we've heard at least five times already (no cell phones). Obviously necessary, that sixth repetition, because only now does a young woman directly behind me admit to having a cell phone. In her pocketbook. But that's okay, isn't it?

The bus driver rolls his eyes; Roger whistles. The guard and the electronics offender exit the bus to register the cell phone in the Wackenhut office, where it will remain for the duration of our tour.

Reading material while we linger: additional prohibitions planted in sand. No pets. No copying devices. No transmitting devices. No illegal drugs. Also a "Desert Tortoise Habitat, Threatened Species" placard.

Sure, says Roger, that "sure" unseasoned by irony. The NTS is "crawling" with wildlife. Deer. Antelope. Badgers. Jack rabbits. Rattlesnakes. "Down in some of those tunnels? You wouldn't *believe* the number of snakes." The NTS also hosts a multitude of "thriving" vegetation, Roger reports, inviting us to guess which vegetation counts as the most impervious to a nuclear blast. No one guesses correctly. "Russian thistle!" Roger yelps. "Don't it figure?"

As we cruise around and through Mercury "camp," Roger lists the service and entertainment amenities of the place, past and present. Five-lane bowling alley, two-chair barbershop, one-cell jail overseen by the Nye County Sheriff's Department. A driving range for golfers, a dance hall, and, in Roger's "day," a "really good steakhouse" that also served six-buck lobster tails.

At Mercury, there are Quonset huts so sterile, so basic, so desert bleached, they could sub for civilization's final outposts. Row housing, every unit sporting the same front door, the same front steps, the same gas barbecue. The desert vista on the left is so very similar to the desert vista on the right I experience a Jessica Lange/*Blue Sky* moment, wondering how anyone arriving at this live/work space can avoid protracted weeping. Then again, military enclaves aren't built for beauty; beauty is a distraction.

We pass Lawrence Livermore and Sandia labs and other pockets of busyness. The NTS might not be the hotbed of activity it was in the wake of Hitler, Mussolini, Pearl Harbor and shoe-banging Khrushchev, but it is by no means a ghost town. The "stewardship" of our nuclear stockpile is one of NTS's current assignments. Another—just in case, just in case—is maintaining a stance of "testing readiness."

At Mercury's employee commissary, we have chance to stretch our legs, use the facilities, and buy vending machine snacks. Until the bus driver and Roger re-board, we're free to stand around gravel spray-painted green and chat with one another or not. When Dr. Jacob Paz finishes his soda, he climbs on the wrong bus (mine). After a few minutes, he climbs back off, and heads for his original transport. Roger sends someone to collect restroom stragglers and off we go, travelling Mercury Highway, the Belted Mountains and Rainier Mesa to the north, Halfpint Range to the east, the Shoshone Range to the west and in between acres and acres of sand, mesquite and the yucca species Mormon pioneers renamed Joshua trees to keep inspiration flowing as they made their way across parched, inhospitable land. Were we to continue north on Mercury, eventually we'd reach (and be turned back from) the security gate that stands between civilians like us and Groom Lake, Area 51. The mention of Area 51 provokes by far the liveliest bus discussion of the day. When the couple directly across the aisle discover I haven't visited Rachel, a town on the "Extraterrestrial Highway," they urge me "by all means" to do so.

"More than worth the trip," the male portion of the couple enthuses.

"Oh definitely!" seconds his partner.

"I'm a bit of a UFO buff myself," Roger declares, then resumes whistling.

Area 5's Radioactive Waste Management facility is listed as our 10:20 a.m. stop. We're skipping that part of the itinerary, Roger explains, because of a "classified ops" in progress. Ahead of schedule we arrive at Frenchman Flat, the dry lakebed area famous for these historic firsts: the first ever U.S. continental nuclear detonation (1-kiloton Able), dropped on January 27, 1951; the first detonation (21-kiloton Dog) observed by military troops—troops positioned, in this instance, a scant 6.8 miles from ground zero. All atmospheric tests were conducted pre-dawn. To prepare, crews worked throughout the night prior to the morning "shot." If the weather didn't cooperate, if the wind shifted, the shot had to be postponed until the following early morning, which meant another full day and night of prep. Which meant—would have to mean, wouldn't it?—countdown by the sleep-deprived.

"Everyone worked long hours," Roger says. "Working long hours was part of the job."

Many of the declassified photographs reproduced in Michael Light's *100 Suns* are Frenchman Flat detonations, taken by photographers stationed at Lookout Mountain Air Force Base in Hollywood.

It is not a book to thumb through before turning off the light.

The debris now visible on either side of the bus is left over from Priscilla, a 37-kiloton balloon detonation carried out June 24, 1957. During Priscilla, 900 pigs, some of them dressed in flight jackets, were blown up (because pig skin resembles human skin). Priscilla also tested the effectiveness of several above-ground fallout shelter designs. The six-inch wall version survived the blast; the two-inch wall design collapsed.

"So you walk out of one of those—then what?" Roger asks.

Jocularly and (surely?) rhetorically.

Regardless, no one responds. To the person, we ride and stare in silence.

At a train trestle mock-up, deformed by Priscilla's 400-pounds-per-square-inch pressure wave, we again leave the bus, the better to marvel close range. The Department of Energy sells an 8"x10" glossy of the warped trestle, but the official photo omits the *BB Bobby Sucks* graffiti. Questioned about the appearance of graffiti at a secured facility, the tour guide from the other bus (Roger has returned to his seat) suspects "disgruntled workers" are responsible.

Disgruntled workers.

Around a stockpile of aging, unexploded nuclear weaponry.

The pile of volcanic tuff known as News Nob, where members of the press, including Walter Cronkite, assembled to witness detonations, is part and parcel of Yucca Flat. Site of 86 atmospheric and 400 underground detonations, Yucca Flat qualifies as the "most bombed place on earth," according to museum literature. From aerial photographs, Yucca Flat looks lunar, pockmarked with subsidence craters. From drive-by perspective, the terrain also appears otherworldly—collapsed and sunken earth in every direction. But the craters we're passing now, in the great scheme of Test Site craters, count as minor concavities. Coming up: a crater 320 feet deep and 1,280 feet wide. Alongside it, we'll picnic lunch.

The Sedan Crater was created when a 104-kiloton underground detonation displaced 12 million tons of desert. It's considered a tour highlight, hence the lingering over lunch. There is a viewing platform. There is a porta potty. There is a National Historic Register marker. When the bus stops and the doors open, like obedient schoolchildren we march forward in an orderly procession. Patiently, without fidgeting, we await our turn at the guardrails and the opportunity to bend closer toward the massive effects of a massive thermonuclear explosion. And once we advance to the front of the line, once we've arrived at the very lip of that enormous sand pit, nothing between us and it except invisible, unsupportive air, some of us turn a little woozy. I'm not afraid of heights; I'm certainly not afraid of sand, but of the Sedan Crater I am very, very afraid. It is one of those visions before which the mind balks. Physically, psychically, historically, metaphorically, it is simply too much to absorb and process.

Back on the bus, most of us half-heartedly picking at whatever we packed for lunch, one of our number jumps from her seat, dashes up the aisle and knocks open the door, shouting over her shoulder that she needs to "warm up."

At midday, in June, in the sweltering desert, warming up happens quickly. Yet for longer than it takes to elevate her body temperature, the woman continues to stand in the scorching sun, rubbing hard her bare arms.

Perhaps I project, but I take this to be an anxiety response. I take this to be an example of the mind, in conjunction with the emotions, exercising shut-off rights. I take this to mean my sister tourist cannot remain on an air-conditioned bus, nibbling on salami with the Sedan Crater in her sightline and a tour guide discussing the aftereffects of Chernobyl.

About that 1986 Ukrainian nuclear power plant explosion, Roger, the retired radiation expert, says with conviction and impressive authority: "Those first firefighters on the scene? They got *fried.* At that level of exposure, your white blood cells simply disappear."

For five hours, we've been touring nuclear test detritus. Our eyes are glazed. Our asses are numb. We are fast approaching utter fatigue of the body. Fatigue of the spirit set in a while ago. We're in a state of sensory and experiential overload. We've been stunned and amazed and stunned and amazed some more, but we're not done. We're still not done.

Roger's theory? If you took a poll of NTS visitors? After they'd returned home? The part of the tour they'd remember most? Besides the Sedan Crater? Area 1. Because, reasons Roger, Area 1 contains remnants of the Survival Town that withstood 29-kiloton Apple 2, one of the detonations "designed to test the effects of nuclear detonations on civilian communities."

Maybe.

But I'm experiencing flashbacks and my tour isn't nearly finished.

We're circling a vacant, window-less house, and I see the house, I do, but I see other images too, images I've added on, superimposed. In archival photos, there's a mannequin in that house, lips red, hair brushed, dressed in shorts, sandals and halter top, standing next to shelves stocked with "Test Program" foodstuffs.

Surrounding the house, I see empty desert, yes, but I also see what once stretched across this strip of sand: a Beckettian line-up of mannequins reared back, spun about, torqued and twisted, arms gone, legs gone, noses missing, their obscenely bland and pleasant expressions intact, if faces they still possessed.

Bright, bright, brightest Nevada sunlight, but I recognize the symptoms; I'm familiar with the shift. I'm falling into nocturnal patterns of fret and fright. Tight chest. Shallow breaths. I'm starting to blur fact and fantasy, give in to swirling dread. I'm seized with the compulsion to reorder information, this bit before that bit and back again in a doomed bid to control and isolate and improve on a meaning I don't care to accept. Little fissures of alarm widening, I'm list-making in the retina-piercing glare.

• Radioactive fission isotopes most dangerous to humans, short-term: iodine-131 and strontium-89.

• Half-life of iodine-131: eight days.

• Half-life of strontium-89: 54 days.

• Harry Truman's reassessment of his decision to drop Little Boy and Fat Man on Japan? "(N)o great decision … not a decision to worry about."

• The "cloud of black dust" that greeted Chernobyl survivor Sasha Yuvchenko when he pulled back the hospital sheets? Dead skin. His.

Back at the security gate, a Wackenhut employee—not the checkpoint guard from this morning but a fellow equally young—climbs aboard to collect our temporary badges.

The bus driver demurs. Badges are to be collected back at the museum. Those are his instructions.

"I was told to collect the badges," says the guard.

"I was told differently," disputes the driver.

"Wait here," the guard says and steps off the bus.

"What's the hold-up?" Roger inquires.

The driver shrugs.

We wait; the bus idles. The other bus is nowhere in sight. We fell behind initially because of cell phone retrieval.

The guard returns.

"You need to radio the other driver," he says. "She needs to come back too, so we can collect all the badges here."

The driver snorts but goes through the motions. Those near enough can hear through the snap and crackle of static that bus driver number one is no way in hell going to return to the security gate. She's already on Highway 95. She's out of NTS territory. Her workday is all but finished. Furthermore, she was told this morning to drop off badges back at the museum and back at the museum is where her collected badges will be dropped. Over and out.

"Yeah, whatever," our driver says to her.

To the guard, he says: "She's not coming back."

Once again the guard disappears to consult with some unseen someone, presumably his superior. When next he returns, he's sheepish, apologetic; he all but hangs his head.

To the driver, he says: "Sorry, man. I'm just doing what they tell me."

And then he backs off the bus.

And then he waves us through.

As if all it took to get around him was persistence.

Scary thought, that.

Quite possibly the scariest in a terrifying day.

Relativism: the Size of the Tsar in Vegas

First light, Wednesday, December 17, we load up and get underway.

On California State Highway 78, we cross sand dunes and skirt the Colorado River. At vista-range, we pass the Chocolate, Palo Verdes and Mule Mountains, all of which the man beside me inspects with a climber's eye and a boulderer's longing. On U.S. Highway 95, near Vidal Junction, we pass, within spitting distance, the famous "shoe tree," a tamarisk dangling hundreds of pairs of well-worn sneakers.

Running shoes.

Escape enhancers.

For the marriage-phobic, any manner of thing can reconfigure as dire portent.

"Feeling a little…queasy," I mew into the palm of my hand in the land of cacti and sand.

"Try not to throw up in the car," my groom-to-be suggests—a genuine plea. Also an attempt to make me laugh.

Success on goal number one, wash out on number two.

Because we left so inordinately, paranoically early, we arrive early—too early to check into the hotel. Down time, fritter time, is not to be desired in my current state of mind. If deprived of continuous distraction, chances are excellent that I will, in sequence: barf, faint and break out in a welt-y rash.

Fortunately, in advance of the unfolding wedding "adventure" and in anticipation of his sister's antsiness on her second wedding day, my thrice-wed brother offered some coping tips.

"You get to Vegas, need to forget why you came, head over to East Tropicana. The Liberace Museum's a stitch."

Eighteen pianos. A Rolls Royce covered in mirror tiles. A piano-shaped wristwatch. A candelabra-shaped ring. Diamonds, rubies and fur—none of it easy lifting. Mr. Showmaship's radiantly pink King Neptune costume, composed of pearls, seashells and bugle beads, weighs in at more than 200 pounds.

Strenuous labor, bedazzling the masses. Impressively strenuous.

The boudoir "installation" features a lighted display of Moser crystal and a bronze ormolu desk. There's also a photo of Liberace seated at the desk, outfitted in a complementary bronze-hued dressing gown. Wisconsin native Walter Valentino Liberace looks perfectly in sync with the bronze ormolu desk. Very likely original owner Louis XV also looked perfectly in sync. It's interim owner Tsar Nicholas II whom I can't quite picture pulling up a chair. But I try, I do try, to place him there—at the desk, not in Vegas.

The Russian component.

It will recur.

In Vegas, December can be startlingly gray, particularly in the mid-afternoon pocket between two and three. It can also pack a sharp and nasty wind. Gray and windy are the outer atmospheric conditions in effect as we exit the parking garage to traverse on foot the last two blocks of our journey to the Marriage License Bureau.

My shivering *could* be caused by wind.

It's not absolutely certain I'm *not* shivering because of wind.

Let's leave it at that.

Although marrying in Vegas is notoriously easy, there remain a few unshirk-able requirements. To obtain an in-town marriage license, both "parties" must present themselves at the Marriage License Bureau, first floor, 200 South Third Street. Both must be at least 18 (and prove it), be no "nearer of kin than second cousins or cousins of half blood," and possess no "husband or wife living." Identity claims must be backed up by a driver's license, birth certificate (original or certified copy), military ID or resident alien card.

No blood tests required—a relief. Blood tests turn me lightheaded and, as has been made clear, this day my baseline lightheadedness already poses a challenge to the keeping on. After a license is issued, there's no need to dally. As far as the state of Nevada is concerned, any couple finished with the paperwork can run, drive or be limo-ed to any of 46 nearby wedding chapels and quick-sign the registry Mr./Mrs.

Many happy returns.

The Marriage License Bureau is part of the Clark County Courthouse, which also houses the Las Vegas Justice Court whose docket includes felony, misdemeanor, traffic and small claims cases. The real estate share guarantees that the steps leading up to the Marriage Bureau entrance are thick with Vegas residents not in the best of moods. (You wouldn't, for example, want to ask any of them, as a favor, to serve as rice tossers.) Whereas the court folk dress in duds befitting reprimand, the marriage license procurers are free to dress à la Liberace. Whereas the marriage license procurers smile and skip, the court folk slump and scowl. My fellow and I, limbs stiff, teeth clenched, seem to belong to the other team.

Because the two of us generally expect the worst and are seldom disabused, we expected a line at the Marriage License Bureau. The roped-off setup strongly suggests that long lines are the norm, very long lines, but only two couples stand between us and the processing clerks. The couple dressed in his and hers glittery gold are cooing in…Russian.

Multiple wall posters warn that *any* error on the marriage license, however minor, invalidates the license to wed. Our turn at the counter, on our official form, we discover multiple errors. Groom's name: misspelled. My mother's name: misspelled. Our town of residence: misspelled (twice). Ominous, that conglomeration of error. A single typo, maybe. But four? One of us nervously licks her lips; both of us indulge in low-pitched cursing.

But on we press, on we press.

By law, wedding chapel reps are prohibited from soliciting on courthouse property, assuring a congregation of that faction a bit farther down the block. When any party of two passes, they leap forward, fall in step and mutter, drug-dealer fashion: "Wanna get married?"

Vexing, that dart and dive, but the query does cut to the chase.

Each year in Vegas more than 100,000 brides and grooms gamble (or gamble again) on matrimony. Not every wedding chapel offers a drive-through option, but several do. Our selection for marrying fast, cheap and without leaving the confines of our car is The Little White Chapel on Las Vegas Boulevard, a "marrying destination since 1946."

The Little White Chapel has a marquee. It has a fleet of stretch limos. It has something like a steeple and a built-in audience composed of idle fellows, leaning on the guardrails of the exterior balconies of the seedy hotel across the street. Beneath the porte-cochere, we wait, seat belts securely fastened, surrounded by various incarnations of hearts and cherubs and cherubs holding hearts.

Rita, window greeter and cashier, appears, shakes an admonitory finger at us and indulgently beams while chiding: "Darlings! This is a drive-*through*, not a drive-*by* event. Turn *off* the car engine."

My groom-to-be (reluctantly) obeys. I go so far as to release my seat belt, but the sunglasses stay put. An armed militia could not separate me from my sunglasses.

After a credit card charge of $65 ($40 for the ceremony, plus gratuity for our matrimonial facilitator waiting in the wings), Rita is replaced by the Reverend Iann Schonken. From (at least) the waist up, he's dressed in a tux. Poking through an opening that could pass as a burger and fries handoff, he inquires which type of ceremony we'd prefer: spiritual, religious, interfaith, ethnic, non-religious/nondenominational....

My almost-groom raises his hand long before that recital peters out.

"Just the basic basic," he says and I concur: "Bare minimum. No flourishes."

The Reverend Schonken no doubt senses that if pressed to spring for further upgrades, we'll promptly drive off and cancel the credit card charge already incurred. If so, he senses correctly. Twenty minutes at the courthouse, ten minutes beneath the porte-cochere, and we're done, not a second too soon. Across the way, on the balcony, one of the uninvited guests has begun to remind me of the boatman on the River Styx.

By catching all typos at the Marriage License Bureau and robotically responding to the prompts of half a reverend, my groom and I are now entitled to celebrate the fact that, in the event of pending or actual disaster, we qualify as each other's next of kin—our prime reason for going legal. And celebrate we do, as only the adrenaline-pumped, nerve-jangled can. Food, drink, an enormous tub, a more enormous bed—we take full advantage of every amenity and then some. It's a splurge, the Bellagio package, but occasionally courage ought to be rewarded, oughtn't it?

The Bellagio hotel/casino/resort is the third of Steve Wynn's mega ventures in mega Vegas. First came the Mirage in 1989. Next the Treasure Island hotel and casino (1993) and, in 1998, the $1.5 billion (or $1.6 billion, depending on the source) Bellagio named for an Italian town on Lake Como and fronted by an 8.5 acre Wynn-made lake. Our room doesn't face the lake and lavish fountains because my climber/groom is a Red Rocks devotee. He prefers a view of Jurassic-era rock over a fake lake created in 1998. I agree with that vista choice not because I'm a climber or rock hugger of any sort. I agree because red sandstone in a desert town is less unsettling than spurting water.

Celebrations of the body involving champagne, sex and bubble baths, however leisurely, can only last for so long, even in Vegas. During the afterglow, we prop on monstrous pillows and commence to channel surf. At some point during that flip-about, my groom dozes off.

Insomnia has no respect for wedding nights—first, second, or (I'm guessing) eighth. Eventually I stop worrying the remote and settle in to watch a two-hour documentary on Charlie Manson and his girl chorus. It's wholly enthralling, that saga of dementia, but it too runs its course. I keep watching, though, through the impossible to read credits. The squinting reminds me that I brought along a book—I always bring a book—but in packing I didn't quite grasp how the tart and twisty Muriel Spark would read in a gigantor bed in a gigantor hotel room. In my opinion (and mine is the only opinion that counts at 2:12 a.m.), Dame Muriel is better suited to and appreciated in an environment that offers up greater surface traction. The other reading material immediately at hand is the hefty room service menu. Twenty-two pages of food possibilities, seven of drink. Single-malt scotch offerings range from $110 to $500 per bottle; blended scotch, $65 to $525. Cordials cost less. The dilemma: if I drink more now, I'm guaranteed to still be awake and drinking while others, refreshed and rested, are digging into their breakfast omelets. I could, I suppose, shove a plush chair over toward the window and, with or without drink in hand, wait for the dawn view. But it's been a fraught day, an overly indulgent night. I'm feeling far too buggy for a sit-still and stare.

Far too.

Back in my bridal outfit of boots, jeans and wrinkled tee, I scribble a note on the hotel's embossed notepad and leave it within the vicinity of a toss and turn. I'm fairly sure that the sleeping one will continue to sleep blissfully through till morning as is his custom, but I wouldn't like for him to wake, discover my absence and assume I'd bolted less than 24 hours into our contract—a conclusion I would absolutely draw if I woke to his absence. Absolutely. We're very well suited that way.

I have no intention of fleeing Nevada or even the hotel. My plan is to roam the immensity that is the Bellagio.

Surely an insomniac can roam incognito in Vegas? Surely to be an insomniac in Vegas is to be in no way distinguishable from the night throngs?

The Caribbean Stud poker table is full to capacity, as is every blackjack table. Legions of cocktail waitresses are delivering legions of glasses of booze. Here and there tourists are doing what tourists do at any and every hour: taking photographs of the walls and each other. Eight desk clerks remain on duty and God knows how many cleaners, polishing marble and glass, vacuuming carpets, dumping ashtrays. An hour later, I'm still hoping the blurred vision of methodical cleaning and frenzied gambling will induce fatigue in the observer. By 3:26 a.m., I accept that stronger measures are called for, widen my circuit, and tack toward the "pool promenade."

New fondest hope?

That gazing at pool water will prove soporific.

I get there—or almost there—before meandering off course. In 24/7 land, The Bellagio Gallery of Fine Art is a rarity: closed until 9 a.m.

Current exhibition? "Fabergé—Treasures from the Kremlin."

At this point, why bother to feign surprise? Clearly, Russia has moved to Vegas. Oh, how I long to entertain my sleepless self with an instantaneous stroll among the pendants, clocks, figurines, picture frames, cigarette cases and Easter eggs crafted by Peter Carl Fabergé and team for Russia's Imperial Family! But that's not going to happen, no matter how pitifully I claw and moon at the door. Other alternatives: remain gazing at the exhibition poster or continue on to the pool.

I continue on to the pool.

Too late.

My overly tired, suggestible brain has taken up the prompt.

My body is stretched poolside Vegas, but my mind is zipping through its storehouse of Imperial Russia factoids. Such as: the daughters of Nicholas and Alexandra slept four to the room on camp beds in the Alexander Palace. Such as: Nicholas called Alexandra "wifey" and she called him "hubby." Such as: Rasputin smelled like a goat. Such as: a special device on the tsar's imperial train prevented His Imperial Majesty's bathwater from spilling. Such as: the Soviets' joke about awarding Nicholas II the Order of the Red Banner in recognition of his outstanding contributions to hastening the revolution.

My groom has nothing against Russia, the country or its history, but prefers a Red Rocks hike to a decorative arts stare. In the lobby, alongside a vase that is taller than the both of us combined, we therefore part company for the morning, Honeymoon Day One.

Far fewer people are out and about at nine than at 3:26 a.m. Quite possibly the emptiness of the gallery heightens the discrepancy, but I find I need a moment, then a moment more, to adjust to a significant change in scale. In the lobby, I was craning my neck to see the top of a flower arrangement, and here, in the gallery, I am the giantess, peering through glass at miniature Fabergé eggs that open to reveal smaller miniatures. The Alexander Palace Egg, commemorating the Imperial Family's favorite palace in Tsarskoe Selo, isn't quite five inches tall and still manages to contain gold, silver, diamonds, rubies and watercolor portraits of all five Romanov children. The Trans-Siberian Railway Egg, commissioned by Nicholas II in 1900 as an Easter gift for Alexandra, includes a silver-engraved map of the railway's route, St. Petersburg to Vladivostok, a three-headed eagle in gold, three Romanov griffins, a replica of the Imperial Crown—and all that but prelude. Inside the egg, the three-section replica of the Trans-Siberian Express is crafted in platinum and gold and will, if assembled, actually run.

The tradition of the tsar gifting the tsarina with Fabergé eggs began in 1885 with Nicholas II's father, Alexander III. Nicholas dutifully followed his father's example until 1917 when the revolution rendered the gifting of Easter eggs passé. Of note: Comrade Lenin recognized the value of the eggs and ordered them stored with other baubles confiscated from the Romanov palaces in the Kremlin Armoury. His successor, Stalin, either more ignorant of their value, more desperate for cash or both, sold off part of the collection to Westerners, a few of the eggs going for less than $500 each. Armand Hammer bought several. Later, Malcolm Forbes owned a few. It's a shame Liberace didn't invest. A Fabergé Easter egg atop the bronze ormolu desk.

Or would that count as overkill?

Also on display in The Bellagio Gallery of Fine Art: the 1896 coronation uniform of the inheritor of the title Emperor and Autocrat of All the Russias, proving that, in the case of Nicholas II, Fabergé and associates worked small for a small patron.

How small? Some historians say 5'6"; others add an inch. Among the non-numeric descriptions of God's Russian rep: "slight," "wiry," and "feminine in stature." A short fellow with short legs, Nicholas II presented best on horseback, excelled at riding, shooting and the social graces, had impeccable manners, and took a keen interest in military fashions. He liked making "fussy alterations…an extra button here, another tassel there" to the uniforms of his favorite military units, according to Orlando Figes in *A People's Tragedy*. As tsarevich and tsar, Nicholas kept a diary, scrupulously kept it, and in it faithfully recorded the weather. On coronation day, on the day Alix of Hesse accepted his marriage proposal, while imprisoned by the Bolsheviks, on the eve of being shot by the Bolsheviks: meticulous weather reports.

The coronation outfit.

An intriguing inclusion.

One almost, almost, suspects Kremlin irony.

Mere days after Nicholas II wore the uniform now exhibited in Steve Wynn's Vegas hotel, 1,400 Russians were crushed to death, another 600 wounded, in a mad grab for gifts dispensed in the name of the tsar. The tsar himself, in a major (and early) political blunder, kept to the schedule of events and that evening attended a ball hosted by the French ambassador and there danced the night away with his new bride.

The new bride: Queen Victoria's granddaughter, future mother of a tsarevich whose hemophilia derived from her bloodline, advised her milquetoast husband to emulate Ivan the Terrible but was herself the pawn of charlatans. When Rasputin's predecessor, a French mystic, declared her pregnant with an heir, her mind and body sought to make good on that prediction with a hysterical pregnancy. Alexander III wasn't an Alix of Hesse admirer; he would have preferred a daughter-in-law who hailed from French or Prussian noble stock but, in this one instance, milquetoast Nicholas stood firm: he wanted Alix of Hesse.

They didn't marry at Vegas drive-through speed, but for royalty they married quickly and with some urgency, following the unexpected death of Alexander III, age 47. A week after the funeral, the wedding took place. Like the former tsar, the Russian people didn't cotton to the new tsarina, renamed Alexandra Feodorovna after her conversion to the Orthodox faith. Too haughty, too severe, Alexandra Feodorovna. And those were judgments rendered *before* Rasputin began to stink up the Winter Palace. But you have to feel some pity—don't you?—for a bride who describes her wedding day to her sister thus: "Our marriage seemed...a mere continuation of the masses for the dead with this difference, that now I wore a white dress instead of black."

Closing in on hour 20 of marriage number two, I'm still gawking at the elfin uniform of a tsar whose real estate holdings would make Steve Wynn's batch look about as large as a wheel on the train inside a miniature Fabergé egg when my prime viewing space is compromised by company. The gallery goer crowding my elbow is not deflected by my here-first status. He's laying siege to the territory: usurp and occupy. For a while, I defend my turf. But it gets old, fighting off insurgents in The Bellagio Gallery of Fine Art in Vegas. Old and (maddeningly, ironically) tiring. So, as did the last tsar, I give in to the inevitable, withdraw from the fray and relinquish my claim.

The weather?

Cloudy with intermittent patches of sun.

Only one task on our dread list remains and my groom and I agree: better to call the relatives with the nuptial news while still within Vegas city limits. Since we warned no one beforehand, we steel ourselves to be grilled, rebuked and perhaps, once the initial shock wears off, minimally congratulated.

Silly us.

Neither side is shocked. Neither side asks how or when or why, pray tell, *now*??? We're half a country away, out of sight, out of mind, and far less enthralling than the projects at hand. My groom's parents are in the midst of extensive kitchen renovations and prefer to discuss countertops. My turn on the horn, I interrupt my mother cooking dinner for a slew of cousins. "What's that?" she asks (twice). "Okay," she says, rattling frying pans. "Uh-huh," she says to someone other than me, then: "Hon, can we talk later? My gravy's about to burn."

Salton Sea, Dreamscape

There are dreams—you know this, as dreamer—that drift from innocuous light shows of form and color toward images less abstractly entertaining, more personally disturbing, images and image sequences with the teeth to hang on past waking, that recast on the retina, demand the attention of daytime, of consciousness, as if simply to throw one off one's stride.

But perhaps you disagree with my take on bullying dreams.

Perhaps you are less disturbed by night's power politics, first run or replay.

If such is the case, consider yourself envied.

Dream elements that unnerve me, during and after: progression thwarted. Non-progression extended. The futility of acts large and small. People and objects in isolation. People and objects in peculiar environments. Unreadable texts. The sudden, disorienting appearance of celebrities and the dead. The emblematic inserted amid the patently commonplace.

Equally unsettling: the dreamer as perpetual voyeur. The extreme primacy of the watch and the watching. The tension of expectation, the tension of suspended animation. The frustration of desire with regard to people and landscapes in that whatever you expect from either will not be forthcoming.

I could extend the list, but why? Everyone knows the irritations of dream. Everyone has felt unhappy, stuck in that night place.

At the northwest corner of the intersection of Highway 86 and S22, south of Palm Springs, within viewing distance of the Salton Sea, there once stood a motel called the Sundowner. I wasn't around for the Sundowner's glory days. By the time I regularly drove that stretch of highway, an arrow lined with nonfunctioning neon pointed at a derelict building surrounded by a parking lot that had cracked open and from those cracks sprouted the makings of future tumbleweed. Still, I was fond of the Sundowner. No matter how decrepit or past its prime, it served as signpost and landmark.

Then came the trip when instead of a boarded-up motel I saw charred metal and ash—a sign, it seemed, of a different sort.

For years I had been tempted to leave the main drag, drive the Salton Sea circuit.

Suddenly it seemed advisable to undertake that detour sooner rather than later.

California's largest lake is not thriving. Ecologically, it's in bad shape, disastrous shape. Saltier than the Pacific Ocean, at its deepest, the Salton Sea is only five miles higher than Death Valley's lowest point. The San Andreas Fault, a right-lateral strike-slip fault, runs along the sea's eastern edge. Over the years, 25 or so species of fish have been introduced into the Salton Sea's briny waters, including the flounder in 1951. Of those, only four currently remain: the orange mouth corvina, the gulf croaker, the sargo (which can be caught using canned corn) and the toughest nut, in terms of salinity resistance, the tilapia, a type of African perch. The tilapia, an algae eater, was brought in to reduce the thriving crop that blooms annually on the sea's surface. In early spring and late summer, as the algae dies off, the air smells rank. Sulfurous. Hellish. A potent stench. Motorists on Highway 86 can smell the decay passing at 75 miles per hour, car windows rolled up, air conditioning on. Sniffed at a standstill, close range, the odor makes the eyes water, the stomach lurch.

The beach surrounding the Salton Sea isn't sand; it's a bleached white collection of the bones and barnacles of millions of dead birds and fish. Although the sea itself appears blue, that's illusion, a reflection of the blue sky. Actually, the water is brown. If you toss a stone into the Salton Sea, it might skip but probably won't sink. The salinity index is steadily rising. If it continues to rise, not even the resilient tilapia will be able to survive. Before he died, skiing in snow, entertainer turned U.S. Congressman Sonny Bono lobbied to save the Salton Sea, where he had learned to water ski. Individuals, environmental groups, governmental agencies and real estate developers have been trying in their different ways to preserve the Salton Sea since the Colorado River overflowed an irrigation canal in 1905 and created it. For two years thereafter, the Colorado continued to roll into the Salton Basin and within that depression its fresh waters turned salty.

It takes approximately three hours to circle the Salton Sea in a car but will take longer if you choose to leave that car, venture forth, engage and interact with surroundings that seem distinctly at odds with Pacific Standard

Time and space. Even with my foot on the gas, certifiably in motion, a day tripper passing through, I feel at the mercy of palpable drag, my momentum severely impeded.

There are street signs that lead to no houses. There are water and sewer mains that hook up to no consumer outlet. There are dead and dying palm trees and palm tree stumps in meticulously straight and orderly rows with nothing on either side of that rigorous symmetry. There are motels boarded up, roofs and walls falling in, partial chain-link fences that keep out neither coyotes nor vagrants. There are professional and handmade real estate signs planted in poor ground announcing one's arrival in "paradise." Plunked among roadside brush are old refrigerators and weathered sofas, cushions unoccupied but suggestive of occupation, as if at some hour of day or night someone settles in to snack and watch transients like myself come and go.

I'm partial to desert vistas. I favor the clean lines and uncluttered balance of a desert composition. I like desert minimalism. I like the ruggedness, the ancientness, of its aspect. Emptiness, in and of itself, doesn't disconcert me. What disconcerts me, circling the Salton Sea, are the artifacts of serial, failed attempts to fill the emptiness and the attempt-in-progress that seems so close to failure but hasn't at this exact moment fully given up the ghost.

It's spooky—as if I've arrived at a scheduled wake a week or month or year early.

Primarily to see and speak with something alive and human, I pull over at the West Shores Chamber of Commerce, an unassuming building fronted by a bulletin board and a fake saguaro cactus. Fewer than half the board's postings are legible, sun and wind having had their way with the words. Regardless, I lean in, peering, trying to decipher the erasures. What I can read without difficulty is a bumper sticker thumbtacked to the top of the wood. *The Salton Sea, The Place To Be*, it declares, but no one is reading that boast except me.

The other car in the parking lot, I'm guessing (hoping) belongs to a Chamber of Commerce employee. The door isn't locked. Entering, I very nearly step on a dog of uncertain lineage and temperament. It's dark inside, a little too dark. My eyes haven't adjusted before a disembodied voice calls from some unseen corner: "We're closed." Not "hello," not "come back tomorrow," just "we're closed." Since I can't, from threshold range, make out the body that goes with the voice, I take another step forward. When I do, the dog rises on his haunches and shows teeth. He'll allow me to back out, so I back out.

No cars or RVs are parked at the West Shore boat launch, but next to the restrooms I find an assemblage that seems to celebrate the Day of the Dead out of season. Two plastic skeletons, tied to chairs and tables, play cards with finger bones. There are empty whiskey bottles and beer bottles on the table, also a rock to weigh down an electric blue tablecloth. One skeleton is just a bare-bones skeleton, the other is wearing a flannel shirt and a bandanna. The dressed skeleton doesn't appear to be the skeleton winning the hand. I take a photo. I glance around. Someone must be having fun with this, but who? And where is he/she?

In 1898 or thereabouts, a fellow known as Captain Davis began camping on the volcanic buttes located near the southern end of the sea. He liked the place. It suited his personality. Once the Salton Sea became the Salton Sea, he built the Hell's Kitchen Café and dance hall. When business was slow, Captain Davis amused himself by decorating his saloon with oil paintings. His subject: the trials and tragedies of the Donner Party.

In the late 1920s before Hell's Kitchen went totally kaput, two Bay Area businessmen developed a stretch of the North Shore using an "Egyptian motif." They called their property Date Palm Beach. They built a pier. They laid out streets. Then came the stock market crash. During the 1940s, another entrepreneur developed Desert Beach. His resort, he announced, was "destined to become one of the nation's greatest play spots." Flood waters doused that dream. The North Shore Yacht Club opened in 1962. Jerry Lewis kept a boat there. The Beach Boys performed there. Then again the waters rose. In the 1970s, a developer's widow opened a casino, a "shot in the arm" for the local economy, the press reported, but it too failed. In decline, the Yacht Club turned into a drug rehab center, then a senior center. Neither constituency remains.

According to a recent real estate flyer, current residents of and visitors to the communities of Desert Shores, Salton City, Salton Sea Beach and Vista Del Mar have access to five beauty salons, four-nights-a-week bingo, one ambulance service, six churches, and "reasonable-priced" housing, starting at $49,000. But I encounter none of those potential consumers. Not one.

I do, at last, spy a house that looks lived in on a year-round basis. Blackout curtains cover the windows in deference to July temperatures that average 108 degrees Fahrenheit and occasionally rise as high as 114. Sensibly, the inhabitants haven't planted grass and their yard art choices—plastic coyotes and seahorses the color of whiskey—look capable of standing up to blistering sun and stiff winds.

But the selectors of those decorative touches?

Nowhere to be seen.

Off Highway 111, at the entrance station of the Salton Sea State Recreation Area: another dog on guard duty. This dog's owner does eventually reveal himself, but not immediately, not quickly. Before taking the cash I hand over to cover the parking fee, the attendant gazes at it as if the appearance of anything green deserves, on principle, his deep mistrust.

When I ask a question, he answers, but those answers are long in coming and seldom recognizably on point.

He hands me a printout of critters to be found on the trail. I might see jack rabbits, he says. If I'm lucky, maybe a roadrunner.

These remarks after I explain I will not be walking the Ironwood Nature Trail, no thank you, not today.

He says: "Make sure to wear shoes. The ground can be thorny."

He says: "Check out time is noon" after I announce I don't intend to camp overnight.

He says: "Dogs have to be on a leash," although the dog beside him is not leashed and no panting dog accompanies me.

I begin to worry that if I don't force myself to look away from the fellow, the dog, the bleached entrance station, I may be trapped in this conversation for all eternity. If it happened, one of us, I suspect, wouldn't notice or mind infinity's constraints.

At Mecca Beach, which I drive rather than walk to, the wind picks up. A hot breeze, neither refreshing nor consoling.

During World War II, members of the U.S. Army's 393rd Heavy Bombardment Squadron flew in from Wendover Air Base in Utah and dropped dummy bombs into the Salton Sea. In secret. For practice. Recalling that fact makes me look up, squinting, into an empty sky. No bombers, no birds either, although the Salton Sea is a stop on the Pacific Flyover migratory route. More than 380 species of birds have passed by and been identified. Since 1996, birds by the thousands have died from avian botulism, 640 in a single day.

Some of their remains must be what I'm walking on, or rather sinking into, as I try to advance. It's an effort, getting from the parking lot to water's edge, physically and mentally. To reach that destination, you have so obviously to traipse on the dead. The blue/non-blue water is indeed brown at my feet, blue at a distance. Across the way, the blue/non-blue Santa Rosa Mountains fringe the sea and the sky. If I could relax into the supreme stillness, keep at the forefront of my thoughts the rarity of being able to swivel my head in any direction and glimpse no one, no one, in Southern California, I'd fare better. But I'm not in full control of my thoughts or my senses. If, through the blue haze, I saw Sonny Bono ski by, if I blinked and a fisherman coalesced, wearing a mask of my dead father's face, I would not be as surprised as I should be. I would just feel more spooked.

Obviously, I could use a drink. Rumor has it there used to be, in and around Bombay Beach, the next beach south, five bars and five restaurants.

None now.

To commune with alcoholic spirits, I'll have to drive farther.

In a desert bar, not far from here as the buzzard flies, I once heard a draft dodger describe, a little too enthusiastically, the "coming" earthquake that would unite the Gulf of California with the Salton Sea. A "fierce tide" would roll westward, across the Anza Borrego Desert State Park and crest halfway up the slope of Montezuma's Grade. In that same desert bar, a former heroin addict—her word, "former"—mounted a tabletop and shouted for the rest of us barflies to "listen up." Her next book would be "a Salton Sea mystery"—when and if she wrote a book.

Cruising for refreshment, in addition to contemplating apocalyptic scenarios and unwritten books, I contemplate this: how easily a person could hide out, get lost, fail to surface, elude the past and snub the future by taking up residence in any one of these desert communities. A person who, for instance, needed to take a break from regimens and expectations of achievement, the pressurized pursuit of continuous self-improvement, a person grown weary of keeping up the keeping up—actuality or pretense.

In Niland, a gas station.

I know there's beer to be had inside because as I pull up to the pumps, a customer who may be a full-fledged Niland citizen crosses the lot and heads down a dirt path toward a line-up of mobile homes, a six-pack of brewskies banging his knee.

The beer from the Niland gas station isn't cold, but it does help counteract a sense of float. A metallic taste in the mouth will do that. Metal: very grounding.

The flea market catty-cornered to the gas station, if not permanent, has ambitions of becoming so. It's tented. The overhead canopy offers shade but doesn't keep out wind and what wind advances. The items displayed on boards held up by sawhorses are encircled and coated with dust. I find a lovely pair of pink sherry glasses, just as lovely after I wipe off the dust, but can find no one to ask their price or to pay.

A dusty wind kicks up and flaps the canopy. Dust blows up my nose. Before I re-cross the traffic-free highway, I absurdly glance left and right, which is when I notice the carrier trailer, its hitch in the dirt, tires flat, a bit farther south.

I make my way over, stand dumbly beside it, dust swirling round us both.

It's a homemade trailer, once painted white, now somewhat painted white, frayed rope holding the gate shut. A house door has slid off the top of the pile. Little wonder. The trailer is loaded, overloaded, with bits and pieces of scraps and crap, splintered wood, shards of plastic, bags, bottles, a green, stained bedspread filling the gaps.

If such a trailer showed up in a dreamed dream, I'd recognize it instantly for what it was: an alert that I was going nowhere fast, a warning that whatever I'd so assiduously collected for purposes of construction and repair would no time soon be put to full, productive use.

Vehicles with flat tires—emblems of stall in any context, but awake and semi-alert, I do realize that this particular example is not emblematic of *my* stall. It's not personal. It has no connection to or consequences for me. It's just a dilapidated, jury-rigged trailer, sitting atop a strike-slip fault, left for now or forever by a stranger.

And yet it spooks, that abandoned trailer.

It and the Salton Sea spook.

In Bed and Out

Work, for the Day Is Coming—
Louise Bourgeois's *Insomnia Drawings*

In 2000, in a limited print run, the 220 pieces that comprise Louise Bourgeois's *Insomnia Drawings*, executed during the long, trying nights of 1994 and 1995 and now part of the Daros Collection, were published in a two-volume set that coincided with an exhibition of those drawings at the Tate Modern in London. Complementing, illuminating and challenging the visuals is text running behind, beneath, across and alongside the drawings, written in English, written in French and now and again written in a mix and match of the two languages.

An illustrated night diary.

Bourgeois's bifurcated response to wakefulness.

Her one-two punch.

An artist throwing everything she has at her adversary—complaint, memory, acuity, pride, passion, doubt, resolve, outrage, disgust—and losing. Losing in splendid fashion but losing nevertheless her private sleep war.

For those paying attention, the 1991 three-dimensional tableau *Cell I* presaged the *Insomnia* series. A single bed, an iron bed frame, a rough pillow done up like a target, the bull's eye where the head would rest—if a head could rest, at night, in sleep. In lieu of a mattress, three separate pieces of fabric stitched together, bearing this script:

Art is the guarantee of sanity.

Pain is the ransom of formalism.

I need my memories. They are my documents.

Already in *Cell I*, Bourgeois presents the bed as a platform conducive to neither rest nor peace, as the captive zone where night and the mind rehash terrors of the past, present and future, as the back lot where night and mind conspire to play rough and rougher.

My reading of the meaning and intent of *Cell I* is this:

Insomnia is a form of claustrophobia.

Discomfort is a form of claustrophobia.

Memory is a form of claustrophobia.

And art, that guarantor of sanity, has its work cut out for it.

(As is always the case.)

By the mid-1990s, Bourgeois and insomnia had been chums for more than five decades, but 1994 counted as a "particularly bad" year for the artist, according to curator Marie-Laure Bernadac. During that stretch of night misery, Bourgeois, Bernadac reports, tried "everything to understand" insomnia and tried to "cure" her own sleeplessness with "vitamins, herbal extracts, and soporifics."

Tried everything, found nothing that provided relief, and so began passing her nights drawing.

As have many critics and commentators, art historian Donald Kuspit, in his introduction to *Bourgeois* (Vintage Books, 1988), stresses the influence of Bourgeois's childhood on her adult creations. She was born in France. Her parents repaired tapestries. Her father was a philanderer. Her mother tolerated the philandering. Because Louise was not born male, she considered herself "an embarrassment" to her father. The bottoms of the damaged tapestries her parents restored were very often torn, Bourgeois told Kuspit, the feet of the figures missing. The young Bourgeois contributed to the family enterprise by drawing feet. "I became an expert at drawing feet.... Everybody thought my feet were wonderful, the feet I restored," she crowed.

If I were rewriting the life of Louise Bourgeois as fairy tale, I would ride hard on those feet.

By her own account, Bourgeois did not have a happy childhood. "You had to prove to your parents that you were worth having," she explained to Kuspit. "This is the world I was born into. It was a very cruel world."

The world both contented and discontented children fear is darkness and the shapes that darkness suggests and hides. If Bourgeois feared the dark as a child, she's since gotten over it. Her response to prolonged darkness as an adult is agitated fury. Like every insomniac, she is displeased to be lying awake in the clutches of night, bargaining with the kidnapper of her sleep. The only way to partially win is to fully concede: get up, turn on the light. By virtue of the evidence that is *The Insomnia Drawings*, we know that at least during 1994 and 1995 Bourgeois refused to be beaten entire. Light on, the artist sketched.

Among the statements made by Louise Bourgeois to Donald Kuspit during their sit-down exchange:

"I am a complete loner.

"I truly like only the people who help me.

"Love is eternal; it's sex that leads to death.

"There is no escape from (your unconscious). No escape from access once it is given to you, once you are favored with it, whether you want it or not."

And: "It is not my responsibility whether (people) understand (my work) or not, only that I express it."

A bit touchy, a bit of a "quizzer beware" that last comment, but Kuspit pressed on: "Don't watch your words," he encouraged. "You have lived long enough to tell the truth." Bourgeois responded to that invitation with a rant on art world "charmers," on museum trustees desirous of being charmed, on the lazy and the stupid.

The interview had gone on a good long while before Bourgeois started in on charmers and charmer mavens.

Perhaps she was overly tired.

Perhaps she was cranky from lack of sleep.

That night is a maze and a vortex, a concentric pressure, a fluidity, a harpy, *The Insomnia Drawings* again and again assert and remind. It is also a cave, a mirror, an exile. As it turns out, self-proclaimed loner Louise Bourgeois has a nighttime imagination drawn to company. *The Insomnia Drawings* abound with pluralities and replications, figurative and abstract. Duos, trios and quintets of flowers, skyscrapers, musical notes, dancing girls, houses, columns, arches, rain puddles, paint brushes, crochet needles, trees, birds, bottles, faces, roots and ripples.

I picture Louise Bourgeois during the nighttimes of 1994 and 1995 in bed or newly out of it, grabbing up the necessary implement (red ballpoint pen, red felt-tip pen, black ballpoint pen, blue ballpoint pen, watercolor brush, charcoal stick, lead pencil) and paper closest at hand (lined paper, three-hole-punched paper, music paper, the reverse side of a Xeroxed copy of Piero della Francesca's blind Cupid, blue stationery bearing her Westside New York City telephone number and address). I picture Ms. Bourgeois drawing rapidly, writing rapidly. Putting the result aside, picking it up, putting it aside, picking it up, putting it aside. And then, by light of day, returning to review what the dark hours had communicated, Bourgeois to Bourgeois.

The Insomnia Drawings favor, almost exclusively, the colors red and blue.

Soothing blue interfacing and opposing disruptive red, the color we assign unrest, violence, jealousy, rage. Shape-shifting water and its links are plumbed. The Seine, Bièvre and Hudson rivers. The Johnstown, Pennsylvania, floods of 1889 and 1994/95. Ophelia, the drowned. Drawn on music paper, no. 59, recto side, a page of continuous ripples, waves in perspective, and on the verso side, an associative torrent of words: "deep well…water can…water marks, water level, water boots…drenched…."

Bourgeois's family left Choisy in 1919 because the Seine lacked the amounts of tannin needed to dye tapestries. The Bièvre River, which could provide the tannin, ran through the parcel of land they purchased in Antony.

"As a child Louise Bourgeois threw herself into the Bièvre River that ran along the property at Antony," reads a footnote to drawing no. 35. Drawing number 35 depicts a young, mostly submerged female, legs dangling above fish and a jagged, spiky river bottom. The girl's head is the bottom of a triangle whose apex is a simple house. It is raining on land; it is raining on water. The footnote does not divulge why Louise Bourgeois threw herself in the river or the real-life consequences of her plunge. The actuality is no longer of prime importance. What matters is the re-creation, the reanimation, of the defiance, how that scene dogs Louise Bourgeois when sleep refuses to come.

By turns blunt, imperious, coy, evasive and willfully inexact when discussing her work, Bourgeois can also pull artist rank and claim the artist's post-creation prerogative of no further comment, as she does with Kuspit. The work is what it is. But in *The Insomnia Drawings*, the conversation, the call and response, the *interview* process, is fully internal. In *The Insomnia Drawings*, Bourgeois the artist ruthlessly interrogates herself with unfair advantage: she knows which closets the skeletons rattle in; she knows where the bodies lie moldering. She knows the mistakes and malefactions of the accused. In possession of the ultimate inside scoop, she uses that insider knowledge to dark-hour hector without letup or mercy.

Bourgeois's artistic response to the self-hectoring ranges from cagey to abject to sneering. The verso side of a red cluster of flowers, one blossom with petals falling, mixes advice with taunts: "Be cool/be relaxed...Little Pretender...Why don't you admit it." (no. 3)

Elsewhere, there are warnings: "Better be ready to defend yourself." (no. 205)

Judgments: "Hysteries are not born they are/made." (no. 17)

Complaints: "Le succès m'exaspère." (no. 153)

Esthetic pronouncements: "Art/est le/contraire/du acting." (no. 48)

Injunctions: "move on—move on—move on." (no. 136)

An abundance of *nots* and *cannots*. On the verso side of a landscape in palest red: "I cannot do more, I am fed up. . . ." (no. 140) On the verso side of four nude females onstage, arms raised high: "I do not play with a man who does not/want to play." (no. 159)

Many are the arguments that circle and swerve:

> why don't you try yourself
> to help them or at least to give
> compassion
> no
> that is
> not my
> job (no. 30)
> -------
> I did not do anything wrong—who said you did (no. 64)
> -------
> I cannot yes you can
> I cannot yes you can
> I cannot yes you can. (no. 3)

Much rarer, the pep talks and self-assurances:

> Believe in Progress, how it is
> possible.
> ...
> Nobody can take my style, it is not possible,
> at least not for long. do not fret. (no. 79)

There is ample evidence of the insomniac's hallmark obsessions: REM and its graphically diagramable rhythms, night and day citations and demarcations, night cautions. "(N)ight: watch out for emerging emotions, hard to/spot out, wait and breathe right." (no. 37) On display, menacing clock faces, a heightened awareness of time's divide: "only the day/only the night" (no. 164); "Night and day/Le jour et la nuit." (no. 165)

There are references to friends, family, neighbors, Bourgeois's lawyer, business associates, doctors, her sick mother, curators Robert Storr and Jean Clair, writers Robert Lowell, Zola, and Proust, photographer Lee Miller, musicians Mozart ("La flute enchantée," no. 17), Chuck Berry and the Rolling

Stones.

There are remarks about the Catholic Church and the greenhouses of the Orangerie in the Jardin du Luxembourg, allusions to the weaver Penelope and the progress/anti-progress of Sisyphus.

There are notations about husband Robert Goldwater, children Jean-Louis and Alain, granddaughter Claire. There is commentary on her Red Room installations of 1995. There is talk of "reconciliation" and "resurrection" (no. 16). Cats are mentioned, rats are mentioned, mosquitoes are mentioned, sinks, drains, toilets and sluice gates are mentioned and mentioned again.

There are mock letters the likes of:

> Dear So and So
> I am writing to say that I miss
> you and that I would like to
> get a phone call from you
> Love Louise
>
> This is the type of letter I ought to
> right (sic) one every night but it is
> easier to make one or 2 drawings
> instead. (no. 214)

Letters addressed (if not sent) to new next-door neighbors in the process of remodeling their apartment:

> Welcome,
> To my neighbors.
> please be timid,
> be careful,
> about banging
> the walls are
> paper thin
> between
> 347 and
> 349
> Louise Bourgeois (no. 101)

On the flip side of that note, Bourgeois has drawn far and farther apart red circles, as if illustrating her petition for space and peace, a visual plea verbalized, a verbal plea visualized. An insomniac soliciting the cooperation of home-improving neighbors.

I sympathize with the operation's point and purpose.

I recognize the strategy.

Begin with a preemptive strike.

Remove all likely impediments—mental, physical, environmental, animal, gadget, human—that threaten a good night's rest.

Plan in advance.

Maneuver, reconnoiter.

Do all that can be done to set the stage for disconnect. Lie back. Hope for the best. And when optimism becomes neither a sane nor tenable reaction to the situation at hand, cease to resist. Give in, get up. Salvage what can be salvaged from a night devoid of sleep: another stint of work.

Counterproductive Bedtime Stories

Before turning out the light and leaving the young and impressionable alone for night's duration, read him or her a violent, vicious bedtime story that harps on the instability of the world at large and the family unit in particular. Sign off with a "sweet dreams." Abandon that child to darkness.

Where is the sense in that sequence?

Where?

Bedtime stories didn't lull me to sleep as a child; they agitated and left me wider awake. Listening to a story made me part of it. Flung among witches, thieves and distressed maidens, *I* became distressed. Would the tormented escape their tormentors? Would rescue come? Would it come *in time*? Fast and faster beat my worried little bedtime heart. Without exception, alarm outlasted any finale. Story done, I didn't feel relieved. I felt tense. Troubled. Disturbed by a narrative I had neither chosen nor controlled.

There are reasons for gratitude, regardless.

As a child, because of the quirks of those who read to me or text availability or simple oversight, I did avoid becoming acquainted with some of the higher-end agitators. The version of "Sleeping Beauty" in which already married Prince Charming impregnates the sleeper (multiple times), Beauty gives birth in her sleep (multiple times) and is awakened not by a kiss but by one of her nursing brats biting her nipple, for instance.

Another for instance: Walter de la Mare's "Someone." Not even a story, a poem. Menacing, nevertheless.

In the poem, at a late hour, "someone" comes knocking at a "wee, small door." The summons is answered by a wee child (why isn't that child *sleeping*?) who, standing unprotected on the threshold, perceives "nought...a-stirring/In the still, dark night."

Nothing *tangible*, that is to say; nothing that frankly *reveals* itself.

Could the door tapper have been a busy beetle, a screech owl, a cricket, a dewdrop? the poem inquires, then feigns ignorance: "I know not who came knocking/At all, at all, at all." An inconclusive conclusion effective in inspiring terror. Out there, lurking under cover of darkness, a dread someone/something remains.

Nighty-night.

Two bedtime standards I *wasn't* spared that subsequently warped my day play:

• "Billy Goats Gruff"

Set-up: a one-eyed predatory troll lives under a bridge. Applicable alarm: every day after school and all day Saturday, I crossed multiple ditches on makeshift, rotting planks.

• "Goldilocks and the Three Bears"

Plot: lost girl enters a home not her own, eats, naps and wakes surrounded by angry bears. Applicable alarm: many, many black bears lived in the woods I wandered.

Kids latch on to stories.

Kids steal first, regret later.

In *The Uses of Enchantment* (1976), Bruno Bettelheim argues that a child perceives the world as "chaotic" and, in response, attempts to impose "order." One such ordering system: dividing "everything into opposites"—which, in Bettelheim's view, goes far in explaining the reason fairy tale characters are presented as either thoroughly virtuous or thoroughly malevolent. No gray areas, no shading.

Nearly 50 years before Bettelheim published his psychoanalytic analysis of fairy tales and folktales, Vladimir Propp, acting on his own "rage for order," in Maria Tatar's phrase, undertook a structural analysis. In *The Morphology of the Folktale* (1928), Propp identified 31 narrative functions and eight character types. Topping the character chart: the "villain."

In the 1930s, when Propp joined the University of Leningrad faculty, fairy tales of state abounded. Disguised as hero, Russia's chief villain tortured and executed "enemies" of The Revolution, declared there was no Ukrainian famine and insisted his wife had not shot herself to escape him. What did Professor Propp think of Comrade Stalin's fairy tales? Or did he very carefully and conspicuously make sure to think nothing at all?

Across land and sea in Franklin Roosevelt's America, my father, one of several sons of a near-ruined farmer, cleared Currituck County swamplands of brush and whiskey stills for $30 a month in the Civilian Conservation Corps, a "make work" program for the unemployed. A few miles down the road, my motherless mother, her straitened household's cook, maid and laundress by default, served up another meal of potatoes to her father, who built, for barter, pine coffins.

Neither fairy tale nor bedtime story, the Great Depression, more than the war that followed, shaped my parents' notion of what to expect from life. They never forgot the hardships and deprivations of those years, never trusted that they wouldn't find themselves in similar circumstances again. Consequently, they were pack rats. The broken, the outmoded, the obsolete didn't get discarded because—who knew? Any and all might prove useful, even necessary, in times ahead.

My father had his sheds; my mother, the attic.

On every trip home, I ascend into the attic to poke about. I start with a plausible excuse (retrieving a lampshade, checking on the disintegration of my vinyl record collection), but it's a sham. I'm up there for the artifacts, the past-mucking daughter of pack rats. Last exploration, I crawled far enough beneath the eaves to knock against a teetering pile I'd missed previously: old books, covers chalky with mold, bindings ripped, edges tattered. But readable, readable.

A pre-Depression textbook, *The Silent Reader* was compiled, per its title, to "provide working material for the development of efficient 'silent reading'" and contains, among other tales, "The Emperor's New Clothes," "The Ugly Duckling," and "Rumpelstiltskin."

In a crouch, I reacquainted myself with the greed, imprisonment, extortion and nonstop tantrums that drive the Rumpelstiltskin saga.

Now the queen lay awake all night, I read.

Now the queen lay awake all night, **thinking,** I read further.

Then I closed the book.

Enough silent reading for me.

The queen had insomnia.

I would rather not have been reminded of the queen's insomnia.

My mother likes to go to yard sales. I like to go to yard sales. A few years back we discovered that going to yard sales was something we could do together without either of us, in the process, overly aggravating or antagonizing the other. After I emerged from my *Silent Reader* session in the attic, we decided to hit the road in pursuit of bargains.

Stop three, or possibly four, I left my mother rummaging through the contents of a sewing basket to investigate a box of books shoved beneath a table. Not the sale's main attraction, books, but a main attraction for me. Snatching up volume 10 of Arthur Maxwell's *The Bible Story* series, I believe I whistled. (Reckless behavior. Whistle at a yard sale and the competition comes running.) In this instance, the thrill of the find was fast followed by a severe case of the heebie jeebies. Flashbacks will do that to a system. The last time I'd touched the shiny blue mylar cover of a *Bible Story* volume, the year was 1957 and I was perched on a bed alongside my cousin Linda, book splayed open between us and braced on our skint-up knees.

In the 1950s, Seventh-day Adventist, London native and self-defined "literature evangelist" Arthur Maxwell repackaged 400+ stories cribbed from the Bible, Genesis through Revelation. According to the series introduction, Maxwell complied his 10-volume set because "modern children" needed heroes other than "Dick Tracy and Superman" to counteract "juvenile delinquency, youthful vandalism, and lawlessness."

As a "modern" child raised Southern Baptist, I was weaned on the Book of Revelation. If a rant gets repeated every other Sunday and squalled nonstop during revival week, it loses its capacity to frighten or interest. It simply does. Verbal descriptions of graves bursting open and contents shooting heavenward left me unfazed. But where words failed, illustrations succeeded. In Maxwell's series, there are far more illustrations than there are stories. The visual rules. In "Good Wins at Last," story nine, volume 10, a red-haired boy in red-striped shirt and khaki pants wafts skyward. In the same drawing, wearing a red sleeveless shirtwaist dress, a young mom (or a female figure I *perceive* to be a young mom) makes the trip with him.

Eventually my mother (still grave-defying at 86) moseyed over to see what I clutched with such intensity.

"Just the *one*? That's all they're selling? Not worth much without the set."

I pointed at the page.

"Remember how much this picture freaked me out?"

She didn't. Or pretended she didn't, as I freaked out beside her.

Of course I bought the relic. How could I not? Bought it, packed it up and shipped it off to California, where it sat on a bookshelf until the sleepless night I decided to dust books. Once I reached Maxwell's volume 10, I plucked it from the line-up, dropped the dust cloth, sat on the floor and gave my 25-cent North Carolina purchase my undivided late-night attention.

The original owner, a Virginian, paid $8.25 for it in January 1966. Her name was Mrs. Estelle Johnson and she lived—or had lived—on Halladay Street in Suffolk. At the yard sale, I'd failed to notice the extensive notations on the frontispiece, flyleaves and title pages.

Insomnia rectified the oversight.

Mrs. Johnson had penned her notes the way people sign casts or the back pages of a yearbook: at varying degrees of slant and occasionally upside down. The majority of entries were dated 1966 and 1967; a few passages had been circled; an additional few had been written in pencil rather than pen.

A partial story, a fragmented story, Mrs. Estelle Johnson's. A story written on and over Arthur Maxwell's rewrites.

Mrs. Johnson recorded instructions on how to clean bathroom walls and where precisely to place the bathroom stool while doing so. She noted the date she mailed her mother a pair of shoes (November 17) and how much those shoes cost ($15). She noted the date of Fuzzy's death, clarified by "Fuzzy is a dog," and also the date her Aunt Bessie turned 71. She listed what she ate on Christmas day: ham, turkey, collard greens and nut cake. She copied down the address of Spencer Gifts in Atlantic City (776 B Spencer Building, 08404) as well as the Suffolk telephone number of someone named "Emma R." She several times wrote and circled the word "hypocrisy" without further explanation. She wrote and circled: "pornography means to burn old books and magazines not fit to read." She wrote near the bottom of a page, in the gutter margin: "The Devil has 2 sermons: time enough and too late."

I'm not certain that Mrs. Estelle Johnson suffered from insomnia, but evidence suggests she and restless nights were well acquainted. "At night I prayed & sang Hallelujah the Sweet Holy Ghost took over," she wrote. In December she wrote: "I got up came down stairs to pray and shout the vain mind down." In March she wrote: "I got up and prayed from 3:30 to 4:30.... I understood the Sweet Holy Ghost to say I gave my best gift, my son."

On two separate pages she wrote the identical: "Heart means not the physical organ But the center of our Emotions thoughts and Wills."

She wrote: "Christ is wisdom."

And then in April, she seems to have reached a point of crisis.

"Went to church at night got a good Blessing Sweet Holy Ghost talked through Sis Harrell I understand Sweet Holy Ghost to say Hold to my word and I will carry you through.

"Went to work the Lord blessed me I shouted in the rest room and when I came home got on my knees to pray tears in my eyes.

"Worked 9 hours MJ took my place Home at night I thought I had said something to hurt her feelings I called on telephone and ask her to forgive me I told her I felt like I did not have a friend in this worrell & no body cared if I lived or die Praise his name Sign Estelle Johnson."

And with that sign-off Estelle Johnson ended all note taking and record keeping in her copy of Arthur Maxwell's *The Bible Story*, volume 10.

If Estelle Johnson existed in a bedtime story, who would she be?

A crone guarding the Suffolk forest? A clerk spinning gold at Spencer Gifts? The palace shoe merchant? A book-burning witch? A divinity speaking in tongues? A magician's apprentice? A scouring maid? A dog fairy? Or Estelle the Devout, awaiting rescue by Prince Jehovah, made anxious by His delay, too anxious to sleep?

Ruth Paine's 2 a.m. Letter

Certain lives, the arcs of those lives, are wildly attractive to storytellers.

The cowardly, deformed Emperor Claudius, Caligula survivor and ruler of Rome until poisoned by his fourth wife, fascinated Robert Graves. The cultural icon who started life as love needy/greedy Norma Jeane Baker entranced Joyce Carol Oates (and countless others). Fiction finessed from reality—and why not?

In Emperor Claudius, Graves had at his creative disposal one of fiction's darlings: the scorned and underrated. Also: the setting of corrupt, decadent Rome. Also: the rise and fall of the mighty. In Marilyn Monroe, Oates possessed a protagonist whose story of abuse, beauty, and beauty abused lent itself to nifty applications of illusion subbing for reality, illusion *overtaking* reality, and worlds (Hollywood/Washington) colliding via sex.

For a tale that trucks in issues of identity, alienation, generational damage, spousal complicity and the political landscape of our planet, 1950 to 1965, a fiction writer could scarcely lift real-life specifics from a better source than Marina Oswald, wife of the accused assassin of the president with whom Marilyn Monroe reportedly romped.

Consider the narrative potential.

- A Russian bride stranded in Texas.
- A dependent who speaks minimal English.
- The too-young mother of two.
- A wife forced to bunk with her mother-in-law.

Other narrative advantages:

- The troubled girlhood angle.
- The émigré angle.
- The day-to-day slog with Lee Harvey angle.
- The sex angle.
- Texas.

Before Marina Oswald became the focus of a grieving nation, before her first husband ascended to the sixth floor of the Texas School Book Depository in Dallas in search of his own story's climax, Marina Oswald, The Fiction, had plenty of raw data to exploit.

"Marina Oswald Cashes In"

In *The Death of a President*, William Manchester listed an inventory of assassination artifacts the widow Oswald put up for quick sale. Title worthy, that impulse/act. Before the U.S. Justice Department intervenes, Marina does quite nicely: $20,000 for her husband's Russian diary, another $5,000 for the Neely Street photo of Lee Harvey holding the 6.5 Mannlicker-Carcano carbine.

In my notebook, I diddle with a chart.

The cashing in could function as starting point or culmination, narrative jolt or plot fulfillment. Marina's personality could be tipped toward pathetic, scheming, or utterly clueless. Push aside the very considerable prohibition that Don DeLillo has already laid mitts on Marina in *Libra* and the enticements begin to multiply.

The photographs

In the published photo archive, she comes across as—what? Somehow not entirely like other girls of her time and place. Blonder? Less Slavic? More delicately featured? In photo after photo of the Oswald couple, he smiles; she does not. Leaving Minsk for America, our heroine/victim carries three daffodils, wears a headscarf, her eyes telegraphing both bewilderment and fright.

What those eyes saw.

What they saw and understood/misunderstood.

What they saw and denied.

A story could be fashioned around the eyes alone.

The warp of childhood, et cetera

The child of a weak mother and otherwise married father, young Marina grows up tolerated (not loved) by her stepfather. She trains in pharmaceutics, flees Leningrad for Minsk, where she smokes, drinks, parties, partakes in White Night revelries, her rebellions small but escalating. She develops a taste for non-Russian, jealous men. Indulges in or refrains from premarital sex, depending on whom you believe. A virginal bride, say Marina and her biographer, Priscilla McMillan, in *Marina and Lee*. Norman Mailer's source in *Oswald's Tale* calls her a woman "always with her legs spread."

Conflict, contractions, a self at war with self: fiction's playground—even before the *fateful meeting*. At a Palace of Culture dance, a semi-vulnerable, semi-virginal, semi-adventurous Russian girl encounters an American braggart who calls himself Alik, waltzes exceptionally well and ever after hogs the plot.

The marriage contract

"I married Alik," Marina tells Priscilla McMillan, "because he was American…(and) had an apartment." Appearing last on the reasons-to-wed list: "I was more in love with him than anyone else at the time."

At the time.

As in: *subject to change.*

As in: *likely* to change.

A post-marital liaison with a former boyfriend, despite the lubricant of French wine, increases the sexual frustration. The former boyfriend turns out to be as disappointingly quick on the draw as her new husband. No salvation or solace to be found there. Back in the cramped newlyweds' apartment, Marina and Alik bicker, fight, slap, scratch and punch, every syllable and sulk recorded by the KGB.

From the August 3, 1961 transcript:

WIFE: You're always finding fault; nothing's enough, everything's bad!

LHO: You're ridiculous. Lazy and crude.

…

WIFE: Don't you see I dust every morning?

LHO: You don't clean up over there on our table.

WIFE: …I washed it twice and you never even washed it once.

…

WIFE: …Alka, do you hate me when you yell at me?

LHO: Yes.

WIFE: Yes?

LHO: Yes.

A marriage on the skids long before the American voyage, Fort Worth vagabondism, émigré infighting and the couple's disastrous decision to share quarters with Marguerite Oswald, a living, breathing stereotype any writer of fiction, for reasons of craft and conscience, would feel compelled to "round."

A Marguerite sampler

"I was…very pretty. I have to say it because I really was…. I was a very popular young lady." *(Oswald's Tale)*

"Marina Oswald seems French to me…. Marina doesn't ring true…. I have to ask myself who Marina Oswald really is.... Now I don't say that Marina is necessarily guilty of anything, but both she and Mrs. Paine have lied, lied continuously." (Jean Stafford's *A Mother in History*)

"I am a mother in history. I am in 26 volumes of the Warren Report, which is all over the world." *(A Mother in History)*

"Moneywise, I got took." (*The Death of a President*)

Vain, thin-skinned Marguerite in black-rim glasses and nurse's uniform, once fired from a sales job because of "intractable body odor" (*Oswald's Tale*), living with a couple fanatical to the point of hysteria about hygiene.

Stop there and you (might) have the seed of a comedy. Continue and risk arriving in less amusing territory: Marguerite endorsing a husband's right to blacken his wife's eye (*Oswald's Tale*); Marguerite out-money grubbing her daughter-in-law in the wake of her murdering son's murder; Marguerite's outrage when actor Richard Burton ("not even American") pockets five grand for appearing on the same TV show for which she, the accused assassin's birth agent, earns a mere hundred. *(A Mother in History)*

"(H)ere is Mrs. Kennedy, a very wealthy woman...Marina, very wealthy, but *I* am wondering where my next meal is coming from.... I need money to carry on...and, as a mother, I think I deserve it." *(A Mother in History)*

Living toe to toe in Texas before "history" found them: a xenophobic mother-in-law and a Russian bride.

America in general, Texas in particular

America disappointed Marina. Texas disappointed Marina. Fort Worth, specifically, bored and disappointed Marina. *Where* were all the cowboys? She had expected cowboys. She had expected to live richer in America. She had assumed, with the change of locale, that she and Lee Harvey would have better sex.

"He sleeps with me once a month, and I never get any satisfaction," she complains to fellow émigré George De Mohrenshildt. (*Oswald's Tale*)

Unhappy, indiscreet, flailing Marina.

The erotic undertones of Ruth Paine's attachment

A 31-year-old Quaker, living apart from her husband, pursues, in the name of friendship, a fair-haired Slavic girl, ten years her junior. Described as "handsome" (*The Death of a President*), "fey" (*Marina and Lee*), as a "quester" and "seeker of enlightenment" by Thomas Mallon in *Mrs. Paine's Garage*, Ruth Paine joins the cast as another unfulfilled woman, another lonely.

She offers Marina and children the shelter of her home at 2515 West

Fifth Street in Irving, a house "almost barren of feminine charm" (*The Death of a President*) with an attached garage so cluttered no one notices the addition of a blanket-wrapped Italian firearm.

The two women work to improve, respectively, their English and Russian language skills. They share the household chores: laundry, cleaning, cooking, childrearing. In this femmes-only cocoon, Ruth Paine, the tireless sympathizer, caters to and counsels her houseguest. Marina, sympathy sponge, whines and fusses and bemoans her fate.

One husband could care less about such fierce bonding. The other, Lee Harvey, sniffs a threat to his manhood, reclaims his family and conjugal rights, packs up wife and offspring and relocates to New Orleans.

Separated, the women correspond. Lee Harvey doesn't love her; Lee Harvey wants her to leave the U.S. *against her will.* "It's hard for you and me to live without a return of our love," Marina writes to Ruth. (*The Death of a President*)

In response, Ruth argues her superior "provider" qualifications. She is planning to divorce Michael Paine. She has her own money, inherited from her parents. She urges Marina to return and live with her in Irving and let Lee Harvey do whatever Lee Harvey wants to do. In a letter written at two in the morning, Ruth writes: "I love you, Marina, and want to live with you." (*The Death of a President*)

In New Orleans, Marina considers, calculates, threatens to leave her husband and finally makes good on the threat. Obliging Ruth drives through the night, Texas to Louisiana, to collect Marina and the Oswald children and, passengers in tow, returns to Irving.

Which is where and when the balance (briefly) shifts.

Back on home turf, Ruth Paine "lays down the law": Lee Harvey is no longer welcome at 2515 West Fifth Street. (*The Death of a President*)

Welcome or unwelcome, he sneaks in one final time to retrieve the weapon his entrepreneurial widow, a capitalism convert, will try to sell on the open market to the highest bidder after his demise.

A Texas bride twice over

Resist every invention, incorporate only the reported "facts," and still from this point forward the narrative veers toward the fantastical.

Marina and children, in protective custody at a Dallas hotel, chatting about Jack and Jackie with Secret Service agents. Soft-hearted Americans sending envelopes stuffed with cash for the accused assassin's non-native widow and children, a $70,000 slush fund, according to Mailer's *Oswald's Tale.*

In a nightmare worthy of *Crime and Punishment's* Raskolnikov, Marina dreams repeatedly of running from a mob, screaming: "Lee did it, not me." (*Marina and Lee*)

Russian in dream, Russian still at heart perhaps, but scarcely a year after notoriety comes calling very little visual trace of Russian Marina remains. New bouffant hairdo, new Neiman-Marcus wardrobe, a business manager to handle her affairs.

A survivor who starts (or reverts to) chain-smoking.

Who starts (or reverts to) drinking her vodka straight.

Who starts (or reverts to) sleeping around.

For her second husband, she chooses a tall man (six-feet plus), a twice-divorced drag racer. The marriage takes place in Fate, Texas, 1965. Three months after the wedding ceremony, husband number two is jailed for spousal abuse. Heading for jail, he quips to the press: "It's just time for her to have some more publicity." (*The Death of a President*) Time served, the groom reunites with his bride, the brawling couple conceive a child, file for divorce and, divorce granted, continue to live as a couple on a 17-acre farm outside of Dallas. (*Oswald's Tale*)

A denouement that so begs the question: of what now does Marina Oswald dream?

Postmodernist possibilities

In *The Art of the Novel*, Henry James discusses the value of the dinner party anecdote in sparking a novelist's imagination. A mere ten words, James contends, are sufficient to suggest the outlines of a fiction. More than ten ruins "the possibilities of the little drama" and serves only to reveal "life… at her stupid work."

In the case of a four-pack-a-day smoker who, after more than 40 years' subjection, still resents the harsh glare of the Texas sun, life's stupid work dishes up on all fronts mind-numbing abundance. An excess of details. A plethora of viewpoints. Saturation levels of both grand tragedy and craven pettiness. Wherever invention might attempt to pitch a tent, reality has already set up house.

Yet a house under continuous renovation.

What happened, when it happened, who caused it to happen, and who deserves blame and/or redemption are all judgments subject to flux in Marina World. Immediately after Lee Harvey's televised murder, she confirms his guilt on Channel 4/Fort Worth TV. (*Oswald's Tale*) Afterward she recants the claim and substitutes another: Lee Harvey was not "the man who fired the gun." Perhaps a co-conspirator, perhaps a dupe, but definitely not the gunman and most definitely not the lone assassin. (*Oswald's Tale*)

Will that semi-loyalist revision count as Marina's final say?

Constrained by reality, factualists will have to wait for their answer. Fictioneers needn't be so patient.

Four Days & Four White Nights

Our itinerary, even for hyper, short-attention-span Americans, is absurd. Peter the Great's city in less than a work week, the red-eye from San Francisco to Paris to the Pulkovo Airport, a hasty check-in at the Hotel Astoria, then back to the backseat of a not-very-late model Mercedes, driver Sergei at the wheel, guide Irina riding shotgun, neither Russian deigning to wear a seatbelt.

We do. Wear seatbelts. And grip the door handles while Irina, turned full around in her seat, provides nonstop commentary. Over the next four days, on occasion, we will also close our eyes, but not to sleep, not to sleep. Sergei takes our full schedule seriously. Tight spaces, traffic snarls, do not deter him. He will, by God, get us wherever and fast.

Any visitor could, should, spend a month in Catherine the Great's Hermitage, another month on a cathedrals-only tour, but we have neither the vacation time nor funds to do true justice to the city of "glorious revolutionary traditions." What we have are four days and four white nights, fewer than 100 hours, total, to take in as much of St. Petersburg's history, art and architecture as we possibly can, to tour palaces, estates, gardens, churches, monuments, cemeteries and museums, to see, smell, marvel and stutter at things Russian and to sample as many varieties of vodka as digestion will allow.

For perhaps the first time in the whole of my life, sleep is not a top priority—a decided advantage in this June city of non-night night.

From 3 a.m. to 3:15, the St. Petersburg sky is marginally darker, but only marginally. Any nap requires drawing the hotel curtains and even then light finds its way around and under the cloth. Not that we're often in the room to nap, change clothes, or brush our teeth. In the few hours we spend apart from Sergei and Irina, we walk along the Moika Canal and the Neva's left bank. We bear witness to the raising of the Dvortsovy Most at 1:30 a.m.; the reunification of that bridge span, slightly before five. In Decembrists' Square, we count wedding bouquets piled at the base of the Bronze Horseman. We stroll the Admiralty Gardens. We circle St. Issac's Cathedral. At official dawn, we gaze up at the equestrian statue the Bolsheviks left standing in deference to its "technical wonder": a horse balanced on its back legs and on that horse a likeness of Tsar Nicholas I.

Bolshaya Morskaya branches off St. Issac's Square, and there, at number 47, until 1917 and unless vacationing at their country estate, Vladimir Nabokov and his family resided. Even before the Bolsheviks posed a threat to the family fortune, young Vladimir was, in his words, a "poor go-to-sleeper." It's possible, when standing across the street from the pink granite townhouse immortalized in *Speak, Memory*, to zero in on the oriel window of the third-floor room in which the future author twisted in his sheets. The bottom-floor windows of the townhouse, now a museum, sport Bloomsday posters. Would the former resident approve? Unlikely. He certainly didn't applaud the entire Joycean *oeuvre*. *Ulysses* he called "brilliant"; *Finnegans Wake*, "a dull mass of phony folklore."

For in-flight reading, I brought along Nabokov's *Lectures on Literature* and, in the hour before landing at Charles de Gaulle Airport, read his appreciative analysis of *Swann's Way*. Of Proust's opening salvo—"For a long time I used to go to bed early"—Nabokov writes with sympathy: "The boy tries to sleep." My other in-flight reading material is a pre-Perestroika, pre-Putin 1960s guidebook to Leningrad filled with such sweeping conclusions as: "The Great October Socialist Revolution...put an end to the exploitation of man by man." Native son Dostoevsky gets a listing in its index, but not Nabokov, who deemed Fyodor Karamazov's creator "a cheap sensationalist."

St. Petersburg, Petrograd, Leningrad and, in 1991, back to St. Petersburg. A city built on swamp and marshland and still infected with swamp and marshland varmints. Above the window seat of our elegant hotel room, a typed warning, in English: *If you leave your windows open in the evening you may attract mosquitoes. A mosquito plug and tablet have been supplied for your use. Additional tablets are available from housekeeping.*

Day Two, after a 7 a.m. buffet breakfast of blinis, mushrooms, sliced cucumbers and seriously strong tea, we meet Sergei and Irina in the lobby and immediately set off for another 10 hours of sightseeing. We gorge at breakfast because we were warned by our American travel agent—and have since learned for ourselves—that if we don't absolutely demand a lunch stop, the Russians won't take a break. They are indefatigable, the two of them, their stamina quite astounding.

"We are moving, yes?" Irina says, whenever the Americans in her charge begin to lag, drag, or dawdle.

Also fluent in German, Irina also works as a translator. She lives in a communal apartment shared by her two teenaged daughters, two elderly women who are not relatives and her ex-husband. The father of her children is "lazy," she says. He is also overly fond of drink. About those living arrangements and the difficulties and indignities they impose, she has become "philosophical." None of this personal information is volunteered. If I ask a question about her work or family, she will answer but she will not, unless further pressed, elaborate. Her grandmother was a doctor, her grandfather an engineer who "saved himself" and the couple's four children by signing the papers that "blamed" his wife during the Stalin era, endorsing the official view that she represented an Enemy of the People. Irina's grandmother was not killed but exiled to Siberia, where she survived but "never forgave," as Irina says, then repeats with emphasis: "*Never* forgave." Irina's parents, who lost the bulk of their pensions in more recent upheavals, now attempt to live on the equivalent of $200 a month. Before being hired as a tour guide, Irina, herself, struggled financially. "But now is good," she says, before revising to: "Better. Is better now"—a woman too well-versed in her country's history for unbridled optimism. As her tone makes abundantly clear, she isn't convinced, is in no way naïve enough to trust, that her "better" will last.

About her city's art, culture, customs, economics and politics, past and present, Irina cannot be stumped. She can discuss at length the 900-day Siege of Leningrad, the restoration of the Smolny Cathedral or President Putin's favorite restaurant on the outskirts of Tsarskoe Selo. She knows the history and dimensions of every statue we speed by. During the Soviet era, more than 200 statues of Comrade Lenin graced St. Petersburg. A mere nine remain, Irina reports, up to date on statue demolition as well. She can converse in depth on either tsars or Communists, and in the rare instance when she and Sergei clash on how best to escape traffic gridlock, it's the route she suggests that seems to carry the day.

"And now, please, we are looking to the right," she says and, like Sergei, we snap to.

To our knowledge, we have incurred Irina's disapproval only once, the cause being our low-end, minimal souvenir-ing. Just as she knows where the good restrooms are throughout the city, she knows where upscale memorabilia, porcelain, fur and caviar can be purchased at "reasonable" prices, products and foodstuffs whose quality and craftsmanship "will not disappoint." But I'm not at all disappointed—quite the contrary—with the single memento I purchase from a street vendor: a set of nesting dolls with Putin inside Gorbachev inside Yeltsin inside Stalin inside Lenin.

Quite warm, the daylight hours. Yesterday, the temperature topped 90 degrees Fahrenheit. The Hermitage isn't air-conditioned. Through the open windows drift noise, grit and grime. I must look outstandingly moist and flushed because one of the attendants, who seems more *babushka* than guard, reaches out as I pass and says (according to Irina's translation): "Come back to us in winter."

Of the Hermitage's 350 halls, 15,000 paintings, 12,000 sculptures, 600,000 drawings, million-plus coins and scads else, we have selected three must-sees and follow the crowd-parting Irina to stand within a nose of Da Vinci's *Madonna and Child*, Titian's *St. Sebastian*, and El Greco's exquisite *Apostles Peter and Paul*. In the Winter Palace section of the complex, we trot briskly through the living quarters of the last tsar and family, a little less briskly through the dining room where the Bolsheviks put an end to the Provisional Government, and then we're off to another Bartolomeo Rastrelli-designed baroque palace, the Catherine Palace in Tsarskoe Selo, a supposedly 45-minute drive that Sergei manages in less than 30.

Much in St. Petersburg proper was restored and refurbished for the city's 2003 tercentennial celebrations, and the Catherine Palace seems to be part of that spruced up, showcasing trend. Ransacked by the Germans during World War II, the palace has since regained its original luster. Very blue, very white, and very, very gold, the Catherine Palace's gleaming 300-meter façade. The famed Amber Room is overflowing with gawkers as we, two more gawkers and guide, pull in our arms and wedge inside.

The heat, our vigorous pace and my lack of sleep catch up with me at the Catherine Palace. I require a moment's recovery. In the gardens we bench sit while I guzzle water, Irina's commentary proceeding without interruption. The lilacs are in bloom, great purple profusions. A string quartet on a nearby balcony is playing "Blue Moon" to entertain visitors passing or sitting. Irina is quite willing, and obviously able, to walk the whole of the park, but we beg off and stumble back toward Sergei and car. Leaving the village, we catch a brief glimpse of the Alexander Palace, home to Nicholas II and brood after the Bloody Sunday massacre turned Alexandra against the Winter Palace. Tomorrow we'll stand alongside the disinterred/reburied remains of all but two of those massacred royals.

It's a bit of a mind spin—and would be, I suspect, even for the well-rested. The Peter and Paul Fortress/Cathedral/political prison and Royal Mint altogether on an island in the Neva. The fortress was Peter the Great's first building project, also where he incarcerated his son, Alexis. Peter's marble sarcophagus lies with five other Romanov rulers, including Catherine the Great. On the other end of the cathedral, in a roped off room, lie the remains of Nicholas II and his immediate family, minus the tsarevich and one of the tsarevich's sisters, whose bones have not yet been recovered.

Imprisoned on this island at one time or another, a who's who of revolutionaries and revolution sympathizers: Gorky, Dostoevsky, Trotsky and Lenin's brother, Alexander Ulyanov, among many, many others. Because prisoners marked for death and exile passed through the Nevsky Gate, the south gate is also known as the "death gate," Irina tells us. It's a lovely spot regardless, overlooking the widest part of the river. On the stone embankments on either side, citizens sunbathe in bikinis and speedos.

Back in the car and moving, yes?, Irina points toward the Sheremetev Palace on the Fontanka, inside of which Anna Akhmatova lived off and on in a communal apartment, plagued by Stalin and sleeplessness. "I know, if anyone does," writes the poetess, "the trails and cliffs of insomnia." "We only dream the cock's crow /.../ the night...goes on and on."

On our own, we've investigated portions of Nevsky Prospekt, but at rush hour we're more than grateful to have Sergei in charge of the navigation. It's crazy out there. A mad dash of man, woman and machine. The three-mile street is and ever has been the city's main thoroughfare. Nadezhda Konstantinovna Krupskaya used to live on Nevsky Prospekt in a three-room apartment with her widowed mother, Yelizaveta. Once upon a time wolves of the lupine variety stalked this roadway. In Gogol's era, prostitutes doing penance swept clean the morning streets.

"Nevsky Prospekt deceives," Gogol wrote in a short story whose main character suffered—what else?—insomnia.

Romanov rule symbolically if not literally ended with an act meant to save it: the murder of Rasputin at the Yusupov Palace on the Moika during one late night/early morning in December 1916. In the cellar of the palace, Prince Felix II and pals poisoned, shot and bludgeoned the tsar and tsarina's spiritual advisor, described in my Leningrad guidebook as the "profligate sectarian priest" who "posed as a saint."

The wildly wealthy Yusupovs owned factories, mines, distilleries, museums' worth of art and so many palaces and estates scattered throughout Russia that heir Felix, fond of partying with the gypsies and dressing extravagantly, often as a woman, was not personally acquainted with all his family's properties. From the outside, the Moika palace is rather sedate. Neoclassical lines, pale yellow in color. Inside, anything goes. Baroque and Empire architecture, Moorish decors, Oriental bric-a-brac, interior decoration by whim though not on the cheap.

Even moving at a much slower clip, we could not take in everything there is to see on the ceilings, on the walls, on the floors, in the foreground, in the background, on the stairs and in the corners of the Yusupovs' Moika palace. There are chandeliers, statues, vases, tapestries, mirrors, mosaics, prints and paintings galore.

From the upstairs' vast expanses, we descend to an elaborately painted tunnel and further descend by means of a narrow stairway. If Irina hadn't been with us, we never would have located that stairway, hidden behind a door that is itself camouflaged by mirrors. Only a few visitors at a time are allowed access to the notorious cellar that was part of Felix's suite of "male apartments." There simply isn't space for a crowd. The first "murder" room we enter comes as a bit of a shock—not because Felix's co-conspirators waited here for the prince to off the monk, but because we encounter those co-conspirators rendered in wax. In the room directly below, wax Rasputin, dressed in a peach-colored silk shirt, sits in front of wax pastries while wax Felix holds onto a chair and stares at the wall to avoid falling sway to the monk's hypnotic gaze.

Edvard Radzinsky, Alex de Jonge, Robert Massie and other historians have described in detail the clumsy amateurishness with which Rasputin was attacked. In the memoir *Lost Splendor*, composed in Paris and published when the prince was in his sixties, Felix offered his version of the event—and it's a sudsy one. In situ, his "head swam," his "ears rang"; he could "scarcely walk." At one point during the ordeal, he swooned. His victim was made of tougher stuff. Drugged, shot and clubbed, Rasputin still managed to get himself out of the cellar and to the far side of an inner courtyard before a second shot brought him down. Still breathing, he was dumped into the Little Neva and in those waters ultimately drowned.

In recounting the city's triumphs, defeats, heroics and scandals, our guide has been scrupulously nonpartisan, nonsectarian, non-sensationalist and dryly objective. But after four days in our company, perhaps Irina is as tired of objectivity as she is of us.

"A great tragedy," she says about Rasputin's murder. "A terrible misunderstanding," she says about the motivations urging that dispatch. "He drank, yes, but the rest...fairy tales."

We are of necessity huddled so close together in the palace cellar, I fear she overhears the startle in my throat. I am trying to figure out how to inquire, without giving grave offense, whether the fairy tale opinion is the prevailing opinion among her St. Petersburg contemporaries when she bolts for the stairs with a "We are moving, yes?"

This time when we speed past the Winter Palace and square where the tsar's Cossacks fired on Father Gapon's delegation, a sound stage is going up.

Tiers of lights are being strung around the Alexander Column. All part of a Crimson Sails event celebrating summer, white nights, and the end of the academic year, Irina explains.

Yes, her daughters will attend the concert, she says, and permits herself a sigh.

They will come to the Palace Square to drink and dance and stay out late and she will call them on the cell phone because they will not call her, and when they answer they will be laughing and they will say: "Yes, yes, Mama, we are here. We are happy. We are dancing. We are having fun. Do not worry, Mama."

—Or so Irina predicts, fretting in advance.

Sergei sympathetically nods. I feel the need to apologize on a variety of fronts, for a multiplicity of sins, because after another long, tedious day in the company of fly in/fly out tourists, Irina is preparing for a longer night in a city where so many have gone sleepless, waiting for children, parents, husbands, wives, lovers, comrades, assassins, tsars, conspirators and profligate priests to return, not all of those granted safe passage.

Asleep but Not Abed

What woke me?

Piss trickling down my inner thigh and a soppy crotch.

But I kept at it, the pissing, until done. At that point, why stop? PJs somewhat pissed on are still pissed on. Never wet the bed, though, not once. From inside to outside I'd sleepwalk, squat and let flow on grass.

When I woke up outdoors—pine trees hovering, field rows laced with shadow, a hide and seek moon in a hide and seek sky—I was never frightened. Finished with pissing, I stayed put, appreciating the night view, letting night air have a go at drying my drawers.

A lights-out adventure, an interlude that broke up night, a fond memory even now, but in Shawboro my sleepwalking didn't make me unique or remotely special. Lots of neighbors, my age or thereabouts, sleepwalked, some with real talent. In terms of superior dexterity, the night-strolling champ was Clark Brinkley, brother of the county's future sheriff. After Clark left his bed, he walked to the window, climbed onto the porch roof and paced at a slant. Occasionally he fell into the bushes but, considering the circumstances, he toppled very seldom.

We possessed the raw material for a B-grade horror flick, the sleepwalking children of Shawboro. A weaponry cache of butcher knives, rifles, shotguns, hatchets, axes and hacksaws. Easy access to miles of creepy-crawler swamp. The protective cover of rural night. Strength in numbers.

We should have insisted (at least) on a school play devoted to the theme.

Then again: why fake onstage what you live nightly?

Sleepwalking, the plot device.

In Vincenzo Bellini's 1831 opera *La Sonnambula,* heroine Amina enters Rodolfo's bedroom during a night walk-about. Despite the excellent opportunity, the count's caddish son holds off on defiling his visitor, so impressed is he by her innocence and obvious virtue. Amina's fiancé Elvino is less convinced of his lady's unsullied purity after discovering her snoozing in

Rodolfo's room. Abruptly, he breaks off the engagement. Distraught, grieving for her lost love, Amina sleepwalks onto the perilously high mill bridge. While spellbound villagers watch, she picks her way to the other side where doubting-no-more Elvino scoops her up into his arms. She wakes. The villagers rejoice. No village crone pulls Amina aside to warn: once a suspicious partner, always a suspicious partner. No kindly onlooker suggests the girl take her sleepwalking skills to market and join the circus. Amina's destiny is Elvino. Curtain.

To the heroine's already plentiful trials and tribulations in *Tess of the D'Urbervilles* (1891), Thomas Hardy added a sleepwalking husband. Angel, rector's son and Tess's true love, is yet another man overly sensitive to female sullying. Tess's earlier seduction by man-of-means Alec torments Angel, awake and asleep. During a sleepwalking episode, Angel slings his naked wife over his shoulder and heads "in the direction of the river," most probably to drown his cargo, since he's muttering all the while: "My wife—dead, dead." He doesn't dump Tess into the river; instead, he dumps her into an empty stone coffin. Thinking fast and in the interest of self-preservation, Tess uses "persuasion," whispering in the sleepwalker's ear: "Let us walk on, darling." Let us walk on. Results? Survival *and* scenic continuity.

Long before Bram Stoker doomed flirtatious Lucy Westenra to walking the night alone or in the company of Count Dracula (*Dracula,* 1897), John Polidori penned *The Vampyre*, featuring an aristocratic bloodsucker based on the mannerisms of Lord Byron, his patient and close friend. On the scene at the Villa Diodati in 1816 when host Byron famously issued a ghost story challenge, Polidori began *The Vampyre* the very evening Mary Shelley began *Frankenstein*, both fictions prompted by a literary dare. The previous year, 1815, Polidori had written a medical dissertation on the subject of sleepwalking. In that nonfiction work, as a man of science, he advised sleepwalkers to issue whips to their servants.

For sleepwalkers who lack both servants and whips, contemporary sleep experts suggest the following precautions:

—Sleep on the ground floor.

—Lock all windows and doors.

—Cover the windows with "heavy" drapes.

—Remove all "pointy" objects (e.g., knives, scissors, ice picks).

—Block off stairways.

—Pad sharp-edged furniture.

—Avoid drinking before bedtime.

—Avoid fatigue.

Or: try hypnosis.

Or: try drugs (e.g., benzodiazepine, antidepressants).

Or: if you're five years old, grow up.

(Most) scientists agree that sleepwalking is more common in children than adults and more common in boys than girls. Several of the activities undertaken by sleepwalkers read like a chore list: feeding pets, washing clothes, bathing, cooking, stripping wallpaper, rearranging furniture. Up a notch, in terms of danger: roving the streets, riding horses, climbing towers.

Sleepwalkers may tool around in leisurely fashion or run that circuit screaming. If sleep talking (somniloquy) occurs during a sleepwalking episode, the talk is generally disjointed and difficult to understand, except in the case of obscenities. Sleepwalkers curse clearly. Although sleepwalkers have been known to urinate in inappropriate places (closets and such), not every bedwetter is a sleepwalker. Nor is sleepwalking linked to achluophobia (fear of the dark)—a separation that makes great good sense to me. If, at the age of five, I'd been trying to escape darkness, I assume I would have sleepwalked my way toward a light switch rather than leave a darkness with limits, a domesticated darkness, for a darkness wild and unbounded.

The notion that bystanders shouldn't wake sleepwalkers?

A myth.

If opera were reality, those *La Sonnambula* villagers could have risked a shout-out to Amina on her bridge trapeze. They didn't, in fact, need to remain hushed and apprehensive, waiting for the heroine to save herself.

Conclusions about which scientists continue to disagree:

—The percentage of the population who sleepwalk. (Estimates vary from one to 20 percent.)

—Whether or not there is a sleepwalking "gene."

—Whether stress causes sleepwalking.

—Whether sleepwalkers are more or less likely to suffer "psychological disorders" than the populace at large.

In *The Promise of Sleep*, William Dement declares that society "cannot hold sleeping people responsible for their actions for the same reason we cannot hold insane people responsible; in order to do wrong in the eyes of the law, the accused has to be conscious and aware of his or her actions and their effects."

When sleep researchers of Dement's eminence argue on behalf of immunity, defense lawyers take note. Sleepwalking as a legal defense (automatism) has been used, to date, in more than 30 murder trials worldwide. Defendants acquitted by reason of automatism include Steven Steinberg of Scottsdale, Arizona. In 1982, while asleep, he stabbed his wife, Elena, 25 times. When he woke, he claimed to have no memory of that violence. In Toronto, in 1987, Kenneth Parks left his bed, drove to his mother-in-law's house, beat that relative-by-marriage with a tire iron, then stabbed her to death. Still supposedly asleep, he next drove to the police station to confess.

Sleepwalking men dispatching women.

I sense a trend.

One wife-stabbing sleepwalker who drew a skeptical jury pool: another Arizonian, Scott Falater. In 1997, Falater stabbed his wife 44 times, then dropped her into the swimming pool and held her head under. To judge by precedent, if he'd stayed with the knife attack and steered clear of water, his chances for an acquittal would have vastly improved.

And what of the women sleepwalkers?

In Springfield, Massachusetts, in 1833, Jane Rider, "Springfield Somnambulist," caused quite a local stir with her ability to thread needles, set the table, cook, recite poetry, pray and sing while soundly asleep. When Yale grad Dr. Lemuel Belden took on Rider's case, her celebrity increased without an accompanying decrease in the incidence of her nighttime walks. Signed into the Lunatic Hospital in Worcester by Belden, Rider was fed laxatives and laudanum. Her head was shaved. Leeches were applied to her scalp. On occasion, she is said to have cried out: "My head, my head, do cut it open!" Belden suspected her of smuggling in green currants—sleepwalking triggers, in his opinion. When bald, drugged and bled Jane Rider continued to sleepwalk, Belden blamed an "irregular menstrual flow."

In a movie, in an opera, in a novel, asylum Jane might have achieved her revenge by laying hands on a needle the size of an ice pick and seeking out her doctor after midnight. The actual Jane Rider, a woman at the mercy of, didn't get chance to exercise that option.

In my backyard, streaming piss, I used to call out into the night. I called to no one in particular. Just called out, to announce or confirm my existence, perhaps to hear my own voice. As soon as I called out, my mother, a light sleeper on her best nights, came running. Having pissed myself awake, I could hear her rushing room to room, frantically searching for me.

Comforting somehow, her accelerating alarm.

I didn't call out again to help in the locating; I waited, in the backyard, squatting, assured of rescue, content. When my mother found me, she took my hand, led me inside and back into my bedroom, stripped off the peed-in PJ bottoms, dressed me in a clean pair and tucked me into bed again.

And then, I suppose, I slept.

I suppose I did.

Beds, a Reverie

1

Earliest coveted bed: my brother's. A three-quarter bed, larger than a 39"x75" twin, smaller than a 54"x75" double, and more exotic for the oddity. The maple bed frame was inlaid with scars, scratches, nicks and gouges, plenty knocked about before becoming my brother's night coach. Like much of the furniture in our house, the bed had been passed along by relatives who had traded up and for reasons of kindness or spite gifted us with their discards. An entire bedroom to himself my brother possessed, another flashpoint of envy. Both room and bed faced fields, not swamp. An expansive view from the refuge of sheets. While my brother was out and about, I'd sneak in not to finger his arrowheads or BBs or bird nests, not even to try on his baseball mitt—tempting pastimes, all. I'd sneak in to sit square in the middle of his bed. I should have realized the intensity of the attachment amounted to a fetish in the making. I should have expected, eventually, that fetish to turn on me.

2

Name every bed you've ever slept in, alone or with company, the spatial location of that sleeping/unsleeping platform, what can and can't be seen from its point of recline, above, below, left, right. Describe in full the cast(s) of light, the angle of shadows. Remember and reanimate the precise emotional tenor of that lying in. It's a game I would win every time. Every time.

3

In thirteenth-century France, the *coute* or *coquette* set atop another mattress, draped with a linen sheet. Very likely my Aunt Clara's twentieth-century featherbeds were also covered with sheets in summer, but I don't remember summer overnights at Aunt Clara's, only winter overnights, and in that season Aunt Clara's featherbeds were topped by blue and white striped wool blankets that smelled of mothballs. In the twentieth century, Aunt Clara's house was heated by a single woodstove located in the living room. To persuade a heat-seeking child to leave warmth for instant chill required calculation, sneaky stratagems. On Aunt Clara's count-off signal, how fast could I race across the hall, leap, dive and sink, sink, sink into the featherbed in the far corner of a frosty bedroom? Fairly fast, and I got faster. One last burn-defying brush against the woodstove and off I'd go. A cold nose by morning, but the rest of my package still snug, still toasty.

4

Egyptians pharaohs recognized the advantages of elevating their sleeping pallets above the damp and drafty ground and made it so; the Romans contributed headboards. The hippie's fave, the waterbed, was an idea recycled. Thirty-six hundred years ago in Persia dream seekers filled goat skins with water and nestled in. The impetus behind the Murphy hideaway? More room to entertain. In the early 1900s, Mr. and Mrs. Murphy lived in a one-room San Francisco apartment. A bed took up dancing space. Mr. Murphy's now you see it/now you don't fold-up design solved the problem without requiring a change of address. Air bed, box bed, bunk bed, captain's bed, chamber bed, daybed, Murphy bed, platform bed, sleigh bed, sofa bed, state bed, trundle bed, waterbed.... A lilting list, the bed list. Almost a lullaby.

5

In Levittown tract houses, the sofa bed became a must-have furnishing. As went Levittown, so went post-World War II America. When our Virginia relatives arrived for a multi-night visit, they slept altogether on our living room "convertible." When snowstorms or hurricanes deprived us of our electric blankets, we slept huddled there as well, breathing in the noxious fumes of a kerosene heater. No power outages, the night eight of us girlies watched the entire broadcast of *Return of the Crab Monster* crushed together on a sofa bed. We *could* have turned on the light when the Crab Monster's mighty claw crested the sand dune, but instead we kicked and screamed and squealed and jumped. It held up well to pajama party abuse, the sofa bed in Shirley Simpson's living room. Shirley Simpson's parents held up well too.

6

It's a story, a scene, a set piece, beloved by Wharton fans. The authoress, propped on pillows, still in her dressing gown, writing furiously in longhand, page after page of brilliant prose fluttering to the floor to be scooped up by the maid and typed by the typist. A good morning's work accomplished before Edith and houseguest Henry James motored around the Berkshires. American aristocrats, Edith and Henry. Jarring, therefore, to enter Henry's guest bedroom at The Mount with a docent guide and see sleeping bags on the floor and a Che Guevara poster thumbtacked to the wall. It was the mid-1980s. The theatre troupe that performed on the lawn slept in-house for the duration of their summer run. Sleeping bags and posters of Communist heroes in Edith's country manor, in Henry's room. Multiple choice: which would have irritated The Master more? A) sleeping bags, B) Communist martyr art, C) the presence of a theatre troupe. In Henry James's failure dreams, there must have been actors, scores of them. I vote C.

7

A bad, bad stretch that urged instant relocation. But where to go and how to get there? Short on funds, I imposed on a childhood friend who lived in a basement apartment in Somerville, Massachusetts. Her wicker loveseat was too short, so I slept on the floor. Courtesy of streetlights, before I slept, between bars on the street-level window, I watched snow fall and the feet of people who knew where they were going be on their way. Before class each morning, my friend dropped me off near Harvard Square where I spent the day evading my future by drinking endless cups of coffee and browsing books. She was a good friend to put up with the uninvited, an even better friend to take on the task of running interference when the man I'd fled began, nightly, to call. I could claim now (and who would bother to contradict?) that I fled the man's bed, a Goodwill mattress on the floor, but that would be an ad hoc lie. The bed itself I had no quarrel with.

8

In graduate school myself, too drunk to drive North Carolina's Interstate 85 safely, another friend let me overnight at her place in town. In her furnished apartment in a once single-family Victorian, she had the beds and bedding to spare. A double bed in her official bedroom, another double, plus chaise lounge, on the sleeping porch, a commodious couch, a sleeping cot. The bathroom was certainly large enough for a divan but stored an overstock of dressers instead. Those nights I stayed over we stayed up talking and, dangerous to neither pedestrian nor motorist, continued to drink. When finally we did stretch out, tired or drunk or tired and drunk, we always left the doors between rooms open to extend the conversation to its last, trail-off sentence. A fine way to drift off to sleep, arguing books and their composition. A fine primer for dream.

9

In the overheated Brooklyn apartment, mice lived in the pot of ivy beside the bed. At night they dug in the plant dirt and scuffled about. Still under 30, I didn't worry about mice infestations or sleep interruptions. Neither kept me awake for long. The resident cat (not mine) wasn't a mouser or perhaps the heat sapped her hunting strength. All day and all night she dozed at the very bottom of the bed, as far from the humans who fed her as possible. If she left that spot to eat or piss, returning to starting point required no great exertion. The bed, low and wide, rested on filched brick pallets. The cat probably didn't care, but eventually I got tired of looking up at a bare light bulb and hung a paper umbrella, painted turquoise with red flowers, above our heads. Gusts of radiator heat set it spinning. The motion disturbed neither female nor feline. When we wanted to sleep, we slept.

10

On Martha's Vineyard, in Edgartown, I first slept at Mildred's Rooming House on a twin bed covered by a plaid spread. Then on a chintz-covered twin across from the Old Whaling Church. Then on another plaid-covered twin off Curtis Lane in the home of two proud Republicans who rented out the upstairs bedroom during the tourist high season. Soon enough, though, I began sneaking down the stairs to share, midnight to near-dawn, the bottom bunk of a bed assigned to a Harborside Inn employee. Always, before either the sun or my censorious landladies rose, I biked back through deserted streets to my Curtis Lane twin, fog rolling in from the harbor. A lovely, lovely ride. But prior to it, in that shared bunk bed, I'd sometimes wake, arms above my head, hands gripping the iron headboard. Fairly blatant, as distress signals go. Yet I paid no attention. It was summer; I was young. Supposedly I was in love.

11

In Asheville, to support my futon mattress, my brother sawed and screwed and bolted together an extra high, extra sturdy edifice. To get off that platform I had to ease off; I couldn't just swing my legs and go. The night of my birthday celebration, a high bed worked to my advantage. My brother got me up the stairs and within bed range so that when I keeled forward I had less distance to fall. Face down, contact lenses in, party clothes on, I slept with my mouth open, drooling on the sheets and the futon. Neither held a grudge. When Hurricane Hugo blew through, I watched its wind effects from that futon. On it, also, I opened the mail packet that contained my first chapbook. On the eve of a California departure, every piece of furniture sold except the futon and a portable TV, I watched, reclining, the Loma Prieta earthquake shake up Candlestick Park. But to California I went regardless and there rode out aftershocks on futon number two.

12

Once, between jobs and homes, I house-sat for six weeks. Answered an ad in the newspaper. Showed up on the doorstep. Came off reliable enough for a pair of barely-weds to leave me their keys and cats while they spent six weeks in Europe. One of the mothers of the pair was an interior designer and had applied her craft to the dwelling. Everything matched. Sofa to curtains to bookshelves to table lamps to cookware to bath towels to throw rugs to toothbrush holders to the toilet brush—all shades of blue, brown, or blue/brown commingled. The elder cat lived on top of the refrigerator but would, for sport, swan dive, claws extended, on passersby. The couple warned me about that cat trick, clarified plant-watering instructions and asked that I *not* sleep in their bedroom, beneath the brown and blue duvet. I was to sleep on the trundle bed in the spare bedroom, along with the younger cat. I promptly and fulsomely agreed, waved them on their way, and come nighttime ensconced myself in their deluxe king-size bed. Deceitful, duplicitous behavior and incontestable proof that the raging paranoia of absentee property owners is fully justified. But for six glorious weeks, my oh my, this girl was one extraordinarily well-rested scamp.

13

For the first four months I shared the Goodwill mattress, my parents refused to speak to me. My (former) professor and the father of two under the age of 11 had bought the mattress following his first divorce. Wherever he moved, the mattress moved with him. During the period when my parents refused to speak to me, he, I and the mattress occupied a dingy, cramped house in Durham County. Instead of curtains, we covered the bedroom windows with Goodwill sheets, further muting the effects of weak, winter sunlight. Weak—the opposite of what I considered my defiant self to be. At the end of four months, my father, not my mother, telephoned. Until that call, we had never spoken on the phone, communicating through my mother, the relay station. "This is your father," he said that afternoon. He never referred to himself as my "father." We're Southern. He called himself, and I called him, daddy. "I just want to know if you're all right," he said, and I said: "I'm all right, Daddy. I'm all right," ostensibly the winner in a battle of familial wills. Except I didn't feel like a winner. I felt like an obstinate daughter who had forced her phone-phobic father into an emotional conversation neither participant wanted to have. And for what? To share a mattress that reeked of indulgences not my own.

14

Georgie Sword sublet her Provincetown A-Frame every winter and took off for more clement seaside towns in Mexico. Smart girl, Georgie. Her P-town A-frame had no insulation. The pipes froze constantly. What warmth there was came from a gas wall unit—very expensive to run. A double bed subbed as a couch, where I could have slept, but on the theory that heat, however little there is, rises, I slept instead on the mattress that filled up the balcony/loft. While living at Georgie's, I typed wearing gloves, slept swaddled and slept remarkably well, all things considered, until the season's first snow. I'd never heard the rake and rumble of a snowplow before. If there hadn't been another, Northern-bred body in bed with me at the time, I would have continued to believe Provincetown had been invaded. The Night of the Snow Plow and nights thereafter, it was assumed that I, a married woman living apart from her husband, was sleeping alone. But that was not the case. For a considerable little while before the Night of the Snow Plow, that had not been the case.

15

Already plenty to ponder: Emily Dickinson's sleigh bed and the "restless nights" she spent there. But one can't help one's associations and where they lead. Covering the poet's single bed, a crocheted spread, its pattern remarkably similar to my Aunt Rosa's guest bedspread, though less than half its size. Because Aunt Rosa taught my cousin Linda and me the rudiments of chain stitching, I have a vague idea of the effort it took her to crochet such a thing of vast and intricate beauty, complicated stitches meticulously interwoven with other complicated stitches (i.e., painstaking labor and lots of it). Two reasons to love and ache for Aunt Rosa. When Linda and I stayed overnight at her house, we were dirt and grit girls; no single bath before bedtime got either of us completely clean. And yet we slept in the guest bedroom and before sleeping roughhoused on that exquisite bedspread without a word of caution or reprimand from Aunt Rosa. Reason number two: she gave the bedspread to the widow her husband, Uncle Herman, was actively courting. A peace offering? A bribe to cease and desist? Unsuccessful, if so. Her rival kept the bedspread and continued to see Uncle Herman for afternoon trysts. "Probably thought that bedspread was meant as a thank-you," someone said, but the speaker was not my Aunt Rosa.

16

A noisy hotel too close to the Massachusetts turnpike. I was sleeping in, curtains drawn, head beneath the pillow. I'd earned sleep-in rights because, the day before, instead of refilling the stock of bras and panties at two discount stores, I'd managed to restock three. The fire alarm catapulted me from deep dream to deep panic, so my grab and dash wasn't well organized or orchestrated. Boots, coat, the manuscript I planned to take to Copy Cop on Boylston Street went out the door with me. The rest of the hotel guests herded outside by the firemen were already dressed for the business day and I among that crowd of the professionally attired: breath foul, hair tangled, hugging a box of typing paper, two feet or so of flannel nightgown showing between the hem of my coat and the tops of my boots. The upside? I now know how the mad are looked at. I will recognize that look if directed my way again.

17

The beds of a grandmother (actual). On the Saturday nights my parents went dancing, I went to sleep in Grandma Dora's bed. Very plain, that one. Simple headboard, hard mattress covered in white sheets line-dried and starched. They smelled divine, those sheets, but they scratched. After Dora, in a snit, moved out of the house she'd raised nine children in and into a trailer parked in a field, on overnights with Dora I slept in a built-in bed of cedar that matched the paneling on the trailer's walls. That bed I adored. The passageway between it and the built-in dresser, also of cedar, barely accommodated Dora's hips. Not that she passed by often. Dora was no coddler. She didn't tell stories, bedtime or otherwise. The bedtime hour arrived and to bed you went, lights off, no "messing." To lull myself to sleep in Dora's non-mobile mobile home, I liked to pretend I was on a train, a sleeper train, going places. I'd instigate a self-induced sway, call out a choo-choo or two for added effect. Never one to tolerate "nonsense," Dora somehow tolerated my extreme attachment to her built-in trailer bed. Who can say why? Maybe she thought she'd lit out for the territories herself, going from house to trailer, yard to field.

18

A grandmother's bed (rumored). Grandma Luna out-birthed Dora by four, turned invalid, crawled in bed and stayed there till she "passed," age 54. My mother scarcely remembers her mother upright, unsupported by pillows. I walked the rooms and hallways of my mother's childhood home the last time it came on the market. It wasn't by then a house my mother recognized or approved of and our breeze-through depressed her, but I appreciated the opportunity to stand in the empty room that had been Luna's and take a bead on the ceiling, windows, corners, cobwebs and dust motes from a variety of bed-likely positions. Never knew the flesh and blood Luna, but my imagination has no trouble concocting a clone. A woman exhausted by children and the hard knocks of country life, a woman enervated by the very idea of rise and shine, much less its reality. A woman uninterested in forcing forward a body and mind both eager to quit. To her bedroom and bed she repairs, never again to leave. A sad ending? Not really. Not to me. And not, I imagine, to Luna.

19

The bed I wouldn't have minded dying in was situated next to a cracked picture window with a view of desert, ocotillo, mesquite and, farther out, Indian Head peak. At dawn, the mountains and the desert below them turned the color of a blood orange. Just before sunset, those same mountains out-blued the sky. In that well-placed, well-angled bed, you could count fly-by ravens, listen to coyotes caucus and, when the wind picked up, to the clattering of palms. Leave the front door open after the rare rain and the whole house, bedroom included, filled with the perfume/stench of creosote. And when night finally arrived, full-on night, you could rest your cheek on a pillow and gaze at a patch of sky so crowded with stars, so saturated with light, it made the darkness of earth seem the sham. A tiny house, built the year I was born, cinderblock walls a foot thick, swamp cooler to beat the heat. Blue floors, white walls, a rafter ceiling. Straw rugs and tamarisk twigs in tins. A hot plate, a mini-fridge, two cups, four plates. A rocking chair painted yellow, a footstool painted green. For whole days and nights, for a stream of days and nights, sleeping in that house, waking in that bed, I forgot everything forgettable, including my goddamned self. But that bed is no longer mine. Bed, view, house—all of it gone. Given up, left behind, parted with in an act of reckless arrogance back when I still could sleep.

Undone: Bessie Wallis of Baltimore

I once planned to write a novel about Bessie Wallis Warfield.

Not the never too rich/too thin Mainbocher-clad Duchess of Windsor.

The younger, shuttled-about Bessie Wallis of 34 East Preston Street, Brexton Residential Hotel, Preston Apartment House, 212 Biddle Street, Baltimore. Wallis of the hair bows and middy blouses and anklet socks who scarfed down after-school meringues, named paper dolls Mrs. Astor and Mrs. Vanderbilt, overly sharpened her pencils, owned a bulldog named Bully and regularly admonished her imaginary friend, Gubby, to "Come home right now!" to Grandma Anna Warfield's house, her own (temporary) residence.

Antic, fatherless Bessie Wallis, Warfield and Montague heir, utterly dependent on the decisions of a scatty mother and the pocketbook of a monetarily sadistic uncle.

That Bessie Wallis.

Oh I had timelines, outlines, a crib sheet devoted to personality traits early in evidence.

Young Bessie Wallis didn't care to share. When her mother, Alice, married the second of three husbands, John "seedless" Rasin, Bessie Wallis protested by demolishing the wedding cake. She "ran hot" in Southern parlance. In mother Alice's description, Bessie Wallis was "an explosive package," mistress of the tantrum. Dressed for a party in a white dress with blue sash, she pitched a fit until the blue sash was replaced by red. Never did she take to being corrected. Thin-skinned when it came to criticism, the thin-skinned herself admitted: "When my mother was going to criticize me, she'd have to lock us in a room together or I'd run away.... I could never make myself listen."

What Bessie Wallis did like to do was compete and, better yet, win. When a kid in the desk ahead of hers in Miss Ada O'Donnell classroom answered a question before she could, she beaned him with her wooden pencil case. Denied her way, she sulked or retaliated with fainting fits. Her voice, even as a child, struck others as very sharp, very shrill. She pestered grownups, asked questions constantly. She was "a handful," "busy as a cartload of monkeys," an adolescent who "would have stepped on her grandmother's stomach if that was the shortest path to her goal." After her mother taught her to cook a Lady Baltimore cake, Bessie Wallis baked one herself. And: "Heaven help anyone who didn't praise her efforts and smack their lips," reported teacher/Mom.

By 1900, the year Bessie Wallis Warfield turned four or five—depending on which biographer one puts one's faith in—she had already posed for more than 300 photographs. The "Wallis Collection," the family dubbed it. Bessie Wallis Warfield Spencer Simpson may have come to her Duchess of Windsor role in many ways underprepared, but in portrait sitting she came with training to spare. The first photograph of Bessie Wallis was taken at the request of her tubercular, dying father Teackle. Gazing upon the result, he is supposed to have remarked: "I'm afraid she has the Warfield look. Let's hope she has the Montague spirit."

The Montagues and the Warfields—Southern clans that turned out judges, generals, politicians and business leaders, but did not form a mutual admiration society. Having earlier exchanged the old world of England for the new world of Maryland, the Montagues regarded the Warfields as upstarts. The Warfields considered the Montagues frivolous eccentrics who had idly watched the family fortune "severely decline" after the Civil War. Areas of agreement: Yankees were a species to be reflexively, virulently hated (Wallis's Grandfather Warfield considered it a "point of pride" that, even after 14 months in a Fort McHenry jail, he'd never stooped to taking the "Union oath") and Alice Montague and Teackle Wallis Warfield's marriage was a misalliance. The Warfields objected because Alice brought no capital with her; the Montagues objected because Teackle, third-born son, wouldn't inherit the Warfield fortune and provide for Alice in a manner to which her ancestors had once been accustomed. Alice got no leg up; Teackle got no purse padding. Monetary objections, both. A never-ending topic within little Bessie Wallis's hearing, among little Bessie Wallis's kin: having or not having money.

As a first line, I wrote:

> *She remembered this about her father: exactly nothing.*
>
> —Because tuberculosis had carried off Teackle when he was 27, Alice 25 and Bessie Wallis an infant.

As a second first line, I wrote:

> *There had been an incident involving stolen jewelry.*
>
> —Because in the rigid spine, crepe-y skin, black drapery pack age of age and darkness that was Granny Warfield, it seemed narratively defensible that young Wallis would fixate

> on and covet her grandmother's sole bauble, a mourning bracelet.

False starts, both.

Next I tried bringing Alice Montague Warfield and Bessie Montague Merryman to the forefront. Two sisters, two young widows, short of cash, trading on the Montague "wit and sparkle" in times bad and worse, providing for themselves by means approved and scandalous in clubby Baltimore. After Bessie's auctioneer husband died of pneumonia in 1901, she worked as a dowager's paid companion. Forced to supplement brother-in-law Solomon Warfield's uneven benefactions, Alice altered children's clothes for the Women's Exchange and served up lobster cardinal, terrapin stew and other gourmet feasts to single gentlemen in the Preston Apartment House. Flirtatious Alice of the generous bust and plunging necklines, the widow who refused to wear widow's weeds, flagrantly scouted for a new husband; her elder by five years Bessie pitched in to help to the best of her abilities and resources, becoming her niece's go-to relative in times of want, stress, crisis and conniving ever after.

Focused on the sisterly bond, I got as far as this:

The Sisters Montague
or: *Schooled*
or: *Charmed, I'm Sure*
or: ???

Sisters. They are sisters. Above all else.

On this excessively humid Baltimore afternoon, in a rented room of the excessively noisy Brexton Residential Hotel, the sisters Montague inhabit poses of utmost cordiality, the mannered surface behind which Southern females pitch their battles.

Fair-haired Bessie sits as straight in the straight-back chair as her corset *(check)* and weather permits, tiny feet in tiny shoes dangling. Younger, fairer-haired Alice lounges in her nightclothes on the unmade bed, her tinier feet moist with perspiration, toes utterly naked.

Proud, proud, proud of their tiny

feet, the Montague sisters. It is the Warfield contribution that has robbed the latest generation of that beauty mark.

Carriages roll by on the street. Church bells chime. *(Something/ something da da; something/ something else da da da.)* In the muggy room, the smell of mold and mildew is stronger than talc, more potent than female body tang. Bessie is thinking about the future and its difficulties because the future is not her sister's forte. Alice is thinking of…nothing much. Swiveling her hips, swinging her legs, she drops her toes onto the shabby carpet. Furry grit rises up in welcome. Eyelids sliding shut, Alice begins to tease the carpet nap with her toes, almost as if she were alone—or the lone female.

Which she is not.

Springing from a floor squat, Bessie Wallis scatters paper dolls. Between mother and aunt, she dashes, miming and mimicking something she must perceive as winsome.

Alice's nonsense, Bessie tries to curb; her niece's, she allows leeway.

"Aren't you something? Aren't you just?"

Doting ramps up the dashing.

If the child catches her toe in the shabby rug, she could easily smack into the bedpost, crack open her skull.

"Bessie Wallis, do stop!" Alice groans. She does not like rush, never has.

"Here's what I think we should do," Bessie announces, as if there had been no lag in the conversation, as if the Montague sisters were utterly in accord. "I think the two of you should move in with me."

"Oh Bessie, honey," Alice says, as if such an absurd notion deserves no further comment.

Bessie Wallis appears to feel otherwise. Mid-kick, she reinvents her performance, drops to the floor, wraps her arms around her aunt's plump knee and shrieks with happiness. (*too much?*)

Cordiality, between the sisters, now stands at its most imperiled. Bessie is merely visiting; Alice is stuck with Bessie Wallis's antics the livelong day.

"*Honestly*, Bessie! Do you *see* what you've started?"

Bessie's warm forehead grows warmer. To avoid declaring exactly what she sees—*especially in front of the child*—she applies herself to protecting stockings from grasping fingers.

But the noise and fumes and *commonness* of the Brexton Residential Hotel are conspiring to override the Montague sisters' time-honored tradition of saying nothing that needs to be said, which at this moment, in Bessie's opinion, is a mouthful. Alice is risking her reputation and Sol Warfield's good graces by cavorting in the Brexton; Alice is forgetting that being a Warfield *widow* is not the same as being a Warfield *wife*; Alice is ignoring the fact that Bessie Wallis is growing by leaps and bounds, a child whose societal debut will be upon them before…

And then, again, I ran out of juice.

As a restart, I copied sentences from *The Loved and Envied*, Enid Bagnold's fictional send-up of Lady Diana Cooper, a Prince of Wales pal who never cottoned to Wallis (e.g., "Wallis wears badly."). I had a notion to use Bagnold sentences as sectional epigraphs.

- Children are young, but not so young as people think.
- The past can be a sad story or a joke—the way you tell it.
- She watched his face, wondering what was going on behind the closed eyes in that bony chamber where sat the little pilot.
- I see how short a time I have to be a woman. You've all your life to be a man.
- Funny meeting a man and then...you find you spend your life with him!
- She's vain but not sensitive. I find that a blessing.
- What you've had you've had.
- Generally in everyone there is something one must fight against.

Wise and trenchant, Ms. Bagnold's perceptions, but as prompts they failed to propel *my* fiction.

In 2011 California, I'd lie in bed attempting to summon up the look and smell of 1900-ish Baltimore with its Chesapeake Bay wind shifts and factory smoke stacks, its immigrants and tycoons. An American city of gas-lit, horseshit-spattered streets in an America of fewer than 75 million souls, an America not yet recovered from the economic jitters imposed by the national depression of 1893. Then I'd get out of bed, go to my desk and be led further astray by late-night forays into the history of telephones and jigsaw puzzles, tuberculosis, dance styles of the early twentieth century, the blacksmithery trade...until even my insomnia-addled brain recognized the need to ditch California-based research for on-the-spot inspiration.

Toward that purpose, I contacted a Baltimore-based company to arrange a tour of the Warfield home at 34 East Preston, the Brexton Residential Hotel, the Alice/Bessie Wallis/John Rasin abode at 212 Biddle Street, Aunt Bessie's house at 9 West Chase Street, the Preston Apartments (if that complex still existed), the Arundell School at 714 St. Paul and Solomon Warfield's Continental Trust Company digs at the corner of Baltimore and Calvert Streets—clarifying that I'd settle for loitering in the vicinities of those properties if access to the buildings' interiors was prohibited.

The company's owner and ranking tour guide responded promptly, but with suspicion. "It would be a big help if I knew what you were looking for," she wrote (information I thought I'd provided) and followed that reprimand with questions. How had I "found" her? Did I have a book contract? What was the "point" of my book? What "new approach" was I using? Why was

I "writing about Wallis Warfield?" "At the request of the Smithsonian, two decades ago" she had "researched and found 22 sites in Baltimore related to the early life of the Duchess," so why had I asked to see what I had asked to see (i.e., sites other than the preferred 22)?

Red and redder flags a-waving.

I reiterated my interest in "young Wallis." I admitted I had no book contract. I explained that my research, such as it was, had led me to her website. As well as I could, I explained why I wanted to diverge from the 22-site standard itinerary.

The owner/guide thanked me "for answering," declared that she "needed to think about how best to help," requested a "day or two to figure it out," and that was the last I heard from Baltimore.

In San Diego for other cause, I made a point of visiting Coronado, site of the North Island Naval Air Station. Wallis and first husband, Win Spencer, one of the Navy's original flyboys, settled in Coronado after beginning married life in equally bright and palm-y Pensacola. The couple met at a luncheon hosted by Wallis's Montague cousin Corinne, herself married to a Navy man.

Lieutenant Junior Grade Earl Winfield Spencer Jr. was (reportedly) an excellent aviator, a raging alcoholic, a crossdresser, and a wife puncher. In Coronado the newlyweds moved house frequently. In Wallis's (ghosted) memoir, *The Heart Has Its Reasons,* the attributes and layouts of houses and apartments are described in far greater detail than are friends and acquaintances. She begins her description of the Coronado house she shared with Spencer on Alameda Boulevard thus:

> It was...all on one floor except for an enormous living room that extended up an extra story. The front door was on the side and opened directly into the living room. Back of the living room across a small hall were the dining room and kitchen. Down this hall were our bedroom and bath and across the corridor...

And on and on the passage goes.

Early morning, while the majority of Coronado slumbered, I cased two of Wallis Spencer's former Coronado homes: an exceedingly modest Encino Row bungalow and the slightly more upscale Alameda Boulevard residence. In the latter structure, once upon a time, Wallis Warfield Spencer had scurried about cooking up artichokes with hollandaise sauce per her Fannie Farmer cookbook and arranging identically-sized fish filets on china plates, the effects of a double Martini not quite tamping down the anxiety that her daredevil husband, executing risky drills in his rudimentary airplane, would return late or fail to return altogether, leaving her, like Aunt Bessie, like her mother, a young, money-strapped widow. If you trust Wallis's memory and memoir, it was drinky Win who launched her cocktail habit, offering up the sauce to steady his wife's nerves on the occasion of the couple's first dinner party. Since Win wrote no memoir, ghosted or otherwise, that particular charge stands uncontested.

While in Coronado, with swarms of others, I passed through the ballroom the Prince of Wales had passed through in 1920 during a locals meet and greet. Standard fare in terms of hotel ballrooms, but the Prince's one-off visit remains one of the Hotel del Coronado's preeminent claims to fame. On his way to New Zealand aboard the refitted HMS *Renown*, HRH didn't linger in Southern California; yet Coronado could have served as the latitudinal/longitudinal coordinates of the future Duke and Duchess's first hand press, eye lock, etcetera. According to historian Benjamin Sacks, that encounter didn't happen because the future Duke's future Duchess was out of town.

As charming as Coronado is, my time there complicated an already stalled project. In thought and territory, I had now ventured beyond Bessie Wallis of Baltimore, opening the trapdoor on husbands plural and husband number one in particular. Should I also marry off Bessie Wallis in my fiction? An affirmative would mean staying with the brat who destroyed her mother's wedding cake, fleshing out the newlyweds' routine of breakfasting on quail and champagne, John Rasin in bathrobe, Alice Montague Warfield Rasin in chiffon negligee. It would mean believing (or believing enough to use) the Duchess of Windsor's published claim that, as a student at Arundell School, "there was nothing" she "desired more fiercely" than making the Captain Ball and basketball teams and—"wish granted"—experienced an "elation of an intensity seldom equaled since."

By extending the time frame, I'd have to cover the angular, square-jawed, monocle-sporting Wally of Oldfields, best buds with "gay, flirtatious" Mary Kirk of the Baltimore silversmith family, a gal "brought up to be as entertaining as one can be." I'd have to include Wallis's debut: the Irene Castle-inspired dress, the drive to the Bachelors' Cotillion in Uncle Sol's Pierce-Arrow. I'd have to deal with Grandma Warfield's death and Uncle Sol's punitive withholding of Wallis's $5,000 inheritance because, in lieu of honoring family mourning traditions, she elected to accept Cousin Corinne's invitation to flee to Pensacola. I'd have to write my way up to and through the whirlwind courtship of Win and Wallis, the Warfields' snooty reaction to the pedigree of the Kansas Spencers, Alice's uncharacteristically gloomy warning that Wallis wasn't cut out to be a Navy wife. And I'd have to wrap it up with headstrong 20-year-old Wallis's first trot down the aisle, November 8, 1916, 6:30 p.m., escorted by dead daddy stand-in Uncle Sol, Mary Kirk a bridesmaid, Christ Church arrayed in arum lilies and white orchids.

But absolutely, absolutely stopping *there.*

Avoiding the wedding reception and Montague cousin Lelia's unencouraging comment to the new bride: "It seems all wrong to leave you here with this strange man."

Avoiding the honeymoon couple's first night at Greenbrier Hotel in White Sulphur Springs, West Virginia, a dry state, where the groom, denied his alcohol, cursed and raged before falling into a funk, a preview of rages and funks to come.

Back at my northern California desk, instead of proceeding, I piddled.

After tracking down a copy of *Some Favorite Southern Recipes of The Duchess of Windsor* (Gramercy Publishing, 1942), I read it cover to cover.

Twice.

The Duchess (or her editor) instructed in paragraphs.

Baked Maryland Chicken

> Use 2 frying chickens weighing about 2 ½ pounds each; disjoint, cut in pieces for serving, wash and dry. Roll in seasoned flour, dip in egg, beaten slightly with 2 tablespoons water, and roll in coarse bread crumbs; place in well-greased pan or casserole. Bake, uncovered, in hot oven (400°-425° F.) for 45 to 60 minutes, or until tender, basting frequently with hot mixture of 1/3 cup butter, 2 tablespoons water and 1 teaspoon lemon juice. Serve with gravy made from the giblet stock and cream.

Giblet stock, giblet gravy. No bait and switch, the Duchess's cookbook. What the cover announced, the content delivered.

Bessie Wallis of Baltimore never underplayed the region of her birth—not as Wallis Spencer, Wallis Simpson or as Wallis Windsor. On page one of her memoir, the Duchess proudly declares herself a Southerner, gilding that lily with: "to be a Southerner was a matter of life-and-death importance during my formative years." Well beyond her formative years, she seems to have made a convert of her third husband. According to Caroline Blackwood's *The Last Duchess*, asked in a post-abdication radio interview "what nationality he saw himself," the Duke answered: "Southern."

Taking a break from recipes, I settled in with a stack of Wallis photographs, infancy through British exile. Despite the portrait training, she seldom comes across as delighted to be in the camera's sights. In two noteworthy exceptions, "the most hated woman in England" indulges in some Southern posturing. Coquettishly twisted on the couch, she's snapped in full-bore "entertaining" mode, legs crossed, toe pointed, one adoring royal gazing at her as if she's the cat's pajamas and then some. A second informal shot shows the nattily-dressed couple on a terrace, Wallis "raring back" with laughter, as they say in the South, the tips of her fingers lightly brushing the bejeweled broach on her suit jacket, a case of having her laugh and bauble too.

Asides.

A dangerous indulgence.

One lead me to another and another until, off the loop entirely, I tumbled into the Hitler nut/Unity Mitford rabbit hole.

As it happens, Unity also inspired a novel.

Originally published in 1935 and penned by sister Nancy, *Wigs on the Green* features the Unity-like character Eugenia Malmains. After World War II rendered both fascism and Unity/Eugenia less amusing, with the author's blessing, the novel went out of print. (Penguin published a new edition in 2010.) Unlike Wallis, the real-life Unity, devoted to the führer, had no interest in marriage to or marriage proposals from English dukes or kings. The two women also treated their broaches differently. Unity swallowed one of hers—a favorite swastika broach—attempting to kill herself.

Pair insomnia with a writing project going nowhere and you can expect trouble in these forms: rash acts, snap judgments, impulsive revamps. The rash/snap/impulsive decision I made one ill-slept night was to plot birth to death. You read that correctly: birth to death. Baltimore 1890s to Paris 1980s when Bessie Wallis Warfield Spencer Simpson Windsor, age 89 or 90, depending on which birth date I endorsed, expired.

For the long, longer, longest view, I needed a new crib sheet.

First pass:

> —**W's attitude toward abdication**: Did *not* weep listening to the abdication speech; paced, screamed and "smashed things" (Source: Kitty Rogers)
>
> —**W's attitude toward boredom**: "I am sure I am better off on excitement—it's boredom that gets me down."

(Source: letter to Aunt Bessie)

—**London fog**: yellow

—**Mary Kirk's contributions**: Catches bouquet at W's first wedding to Win; introduces W to Ernest Simpson in New York (1926); marries Ernest herself after he and W divorce

—**W's (grown-up) temper:** "Furious when crossed… wild when angry…no end to her hate or temper." (Source: Ernest Simpson)

—**W masters the art of the curtsey**: on train to Fort Belvedere

—**State of W's (grown-up) "nerves"**: "She never stopped moving...jumping up to pouf a cushion, center flowers, empty ashtrays." (Source: Duchess of Marlborough)

—**W's (grown-up) language**: "Can you *believe* it?"—"Can you beat it?"—"You know how I go to pieces."—"Wasn't it all terrible, pathetic and tragic?"—"Wouldn't Mother have loved it all?" (Source: letters to Aunt Bessie)

—**On pleasing the Prince of Wales/King Edward VIII/Duke of Windsor**: "It's trying…the tiny brain works overtime." (Source: letter to Aunt Bessie)

—**Sleep habits**: As Duchess, four hours a night

—**In "exile"**: Nazi sympathizer

—**Beginning of decline**: Facelifts, mini-skirts, dancing The Twist in NYC nightclub

—**Finale:** Bois de Boulogne (Boulogne Forest), Paris

In a rented villa, Bessie Wallis of Baltimore met her end as the Duchess of Windsor, physically paralyzed, money paranoid, bed-confined, her household, meds and dying controlled by lawyer/executrix Maître Blum.

A woman with fewer fans than the Duchess of Windsor, Suzanne Blum was someone, I'm fairly sure, even the South would judge peculiar. A supremely vindictive force of nature, she managed to cow the un-cowardly likes of Lady Caroline Blackwood and Lady Diana Mosley. Her attachment to the Duchess was…extreme. Among other weirdnesses, she insisted Wallis died a virgin. In charge of the goings on at the Windsor Villa in the Bois, Blum convinced the enfeebled, widowed Duchess that she was going broke (not the case), cut off Wallis's vodka supply early in the game, drastically reduced staff, forbade flower arrangements (too expensive), barred visitors (because they "raised the Duchess's blood pressure") and left her client to go further gaga in a dark room. Whether Maître Blum was or wasn't aware that the only rival to Wallis's lifelong fear of penury was her lifelong fear of the dark becomes, therefore, not an idle question. As the invalid wasted away in an upper bedroom, a feeder tube in her nose, "something gone horribly wrong with her sad little hands" in Lady Mosley's phrase, outside the once grand mansion weeds grew weedier, trees rotted, branches fell, home and gardens deteriorating in stride with its nominal mistress.

There's more than a whiff of fairy tale in that locked gate/brambled setting, in the increasingly unequal combat between the bewitcher of kings from Baltimore and her fierce, jealous Parisian keeper. With or without the fairy tale flourishes, a novel could be composed by someone who wouldn't shy away from an agitated character trapped by night and other guardians in a holding pen bed, a sheeted cage.

But I'm not that someone, I've had to concede.

My Bessie Wallis novel wouldn't fly; it simply wouldn't fly.

Among the Wakeful, These

The house I now live in—not the house with the sea lion chorus, not the house with the bedroom invaded by phantoms—was built on a plot of land that slopes, on a street that dead-ends. Even so, it's a lengthy street, straight stretches interspersed with sudden, gnarly turns. My house is located near the beginning of the street, which means cars headed toward or away from the majority of driveways in the neighborhood are either accelerating after the intersection stop sign or braking in advance of same. My current bedroom faces the street, an arrangement dictated by architecture rather than choice. Whatever the hour, night or day, whether the windows are open or shut, in that room I hear street traffic. Unavoidable, unremarkable, generic noise until one passerby distinguished itself from the pack.

Probably I wouldn't have noticed the exception had I been sleeping.

But of course I wasn't sleeping.

I was awake, listening to traffic.

Night after night after night, six nights of seven, between 3:11 and 3:14 a.m., a particular car approached and departed my hearing zone. It never passed my house earlier than 3:11 a.m., never later than 3:14 a.m., and never at any hour on Sunday. I didn't see the car; I recognized it by sound. This car travelled very, very slowly. Unlike the usual late night/early morning drive-bys, it didn't speed up after turning onto the street or take the curve, brakes screeching. It chugged and poked along. The engine needed a tune-up; the muffler needed replacing. But it made its way regardless, coming and going to come again.

I began to think of it, refer to it, as the "night trawler"—night being fluid, car being boat, night and metaphor being chums. I also became overly attached. Once I began to expect the night trawler, I began to count on its coming. And once I began to count on its coming, I began to anticipate the event. Initially, during the wait, I'd check the clock. But I soon stopped that. Again and again, the night trawler proved true, arriving, departing, focusing my attention, dividing the darkness, defining how much of night lay behind, how much ahead, offering an outsider's calculation of the hours, minutes and tick-tocks between me and dawn.

The first time the chug-along went missing, I reacted like a lover whose assignation had gone awry. Lying in bed, I strained to hear what wasn't there to hear, worked hard to convince myself I'd heard what I hadn't. Then I got out of bed, raised the blinds, peered past clumps of oleander and boxwood. No cars. Nothing in motion. Not even a grubbing raccoon. Window to window, I went to be greeted by different angles of the same absence. Eventually I opened the front door, stepped into night air and cocked an ear toward the street, thinking to improve audial transmission. Still no night trawler or night trawler echo.

The ferocity of my disappointment—you can't conceive! (Or perhaps you can?) However gravely disappointed, I didn't for an instant imagine the night trawler out of commission—marooned in a parking lot or hauled to a repair shop or retired to permanent storage. No, no. I had every faith, *every faith* that it continued its journeys elsewhere, engine knocking, progress slow but steady.

Just not in my neighborhood.

Just not on my night street.

A telling reaction, that. An insomniac's conclusion. Jilted by sleep, the sleepless assume themselves in line for similar heartache from multiple sources.

A suspicion the night trawler episode confirmed, did it not?

*

Generations of organists have performed for God and community at Providence Baptist Church in Shawboro, North Carolina, including, in my time, one named Walter. Red-haired Walter had a redhead's pale complexion, chubby arms and infinite diffidence. Whichever hymns the choir director demanded he play, he played without hesitation, argument or counter-suggestion, seemingly unperturbed by autocratic rule. When teased by kids or adults, Walter's cheeks flamed, yet the sum of him remained affable, no temper in evidence. He lived with his sister in their childhood home, a two-story, multiple-porches house on Gregory Road, not far from the grain bins. His sister had been married but was no longer. Walter, never a groom. Whatever funds the pair lived on, they had inherited along with the house. Playing the organ for Providence Baptist Church was a non-paying gig.

After Walter resigned as organist—"nerves" offered as cause—he and his sister kept close to home. They continued to mow their lawn, continued to pick up the oak limbs strewn about during hurricane season, hired house-painters before mold and mildew infestations turned the clapboard too dingy, kept up their property to community standards in every aspect. But the inhabitants themselves: rarely seen out and about, together or apart.

"Anyone heard anything from Walter or his sister?' was a question typically followed by a quick tally and anecdotal, if not bankable, evidence that Walter and his sister were "all right," neither of them dead and putrefying in the shut-up house.

The sister's pleasures and habits? A mystery. Walter's post-organist day schedule? Also a mystery. But at night Walter liked to stroll—up and down Gregory Road and farther. He wasn't sleepwalking. During those nocturnal rambles, he didn't wear pajamas. He dressed semi-formally (white shirt, dress slacks). He didn't use a flashlight; he got by on whatever illumination the moon did or didn't provide, darkness not one of the conditions that agitated Walter's nerves. It was Walter, suddenly revealed in the flare of headlights, loping along the weedy embankment past midnight, who caused the conniptions. Folks would think they were driving a deserted road and then, boom, there he'd be. Ghostly pale Walter.

"For a minute I didn't know *what* was coming at me. And that's the gospel truth," it was said often, by many.

A temporary confusion. Everyone eventually recognized Walter and stopped to ask whether he needed a ride back to his house or somewhere else, all such offers diffidently refused.

Walter didn't care to ride; he wanted to walk the night.

George Lindenburger Van Bibber IV, born 1906, lifelong bachelor and resident of Bel Air, Maryland, donated to the Maryland Historical Society Library in Baltimore upon his death, April 1979, the following personal artifacts: his watercolor sketches, his scrapbooks, stacks of annotated newspaper clippings, a treatise on grammar, several volumes of unpublished poetry, more than several boxes of personal correspondence, miscellaneous souvenirs from Panama, Japan, Havana and Mexico City, seven travel journals, and a 63-volume diary of some 50,000 pages that chronicled the events and non-events of days and nights spent closer to home. He recorded, for instance:

When he washed his socks.

When and how often he shaved.

How much sherry he drank.

When he neglected to bathe.

Whom he passed on the street.

What he ate for supper. (Chipped beef and baked custard on a regular basis.)

Where he bought his Panama hats.

Why Prohibition was evil.

Quotes reflecting optimism.

Quotes reflecting pessimism.

Van Bibber began his diary project as an undergraduate at the University of Virginia. Not the best of spellers, he wrote phonetically before devising his own system of shorthand. Later, he made entries in Russian. Later still, he invented his own alphabet.

Degree in architecture completed, he returned home to live with his mother. For the next 24 years, he worked as a draftsman. Following his mother's death in 1955, he began renting out rooms to boarders and "taking his meals in the restaurants and cafes of Bel Air," according to the library's descriptive summary. "This habit ensured that Van Bibber was a familiar personage in town and his diaries are full of references to pedestrians and motorists hailed during his perambulations."

Walker by day, diarist by night.

The less he slept, the more he scribbled.

Van Bibber first began to experience trouble sleeping in his twenties, around the time he launched his diary. Early entries complain of sleep interrupted, of an inability to "sleep well in the early morning," of nights when he "would have slept but for a buzzing fly."

Would have, did not.

An "exuberant" drinker in his youth, Van Bibber drank harder as he aged. After a 1968 binge landed him in the hospital, he resolved to give up alcohol entirely. Whenever he welshed on that vow, he admitted as much to his diary, recording the hour(s) he tippled, the kind(s) of liquor imbibed, and precisely how much of it went down his throat.

A backslider, but no liar, George Lindenburger Van Bibber IV.

Pesky flies, alcohol consumed or strenuously avoided, the obsessive/compulsive need to record the repetitive minutiae of one's existence—insomnia's play pals, every one.

In his next to last diary entry, dated February 26, 1979, Van Bibber resolved once more to quit drinking, conceding that he "cudnt kEp it up." He set himself a timeline, allotted "a wEk in which 2rEali quit."

A resolution with conditions.

First he had "2 finish last botl id stRtd."

Final word, final entry, February 27, is reserved for the other agony: "awOk."

*

Like Maryland's Van Bibber, Currituck County, North Carolina's W.T. Griggs was a University of Virginia graduate, lifelong bachelor and son returned home. A country doc who started practicing medicine in the nineteenth century and continued 50-odd years into the twentieth. A man on the job seven days and nights a week, treating the ills of farmers, fishermen, tradesmen and their kin throughout the Currituck peninsula and in the beach villages clustered across the water, on the other side of Currituck Sound. Until 1913, for his mainland transportation, he used a horse and buggy. That year, Dr. Griggs shelled out for a Ford.

The doctor himself didn't drive. While his driver negotiated dusty, rutted, muddy, washed out, icy roads, Dr. Griggs catnapped. Whenever the driver spied a white rag tied to a gatepost by day, a lantern lit and hung on a fence by night, he pulled over, cut the engine and woke his boss.

Miles logged on the road per month: 3,500 (give or take a country mile).

Career total of babies home delivered: 4,000 (give or take a young'un or two).

Typhoid vaccinations administered in the dangerously infectious year of 1934: 1,600 (one self-administered, a heal-thyself practitioner).

Rarely did the doctor sleep more than four hours of any given 24. And there were exceptions. Always exceptions.

"I remember a period of five weeks during an epidemic," the doctor mused to a cub reporter in 1936, "when I hardly had time to take off my clothes."

Informed late on a blustery winter's day that a hunting guide "had shot his arm to pieces," the doctor and three men set off across the frozen Currituck Sound. It took the efforts of all four to get the boat through the ice to the other shore. Once the doctor reached his patient, he amputated the guide's arm to save his life. Surgery finished, in the small hours of a new morning, doctor and team fetched their boat and shoved it the five miles home.

During the thaw months, when crossing the Currituck Sound, the doctor stretched out on a pallet wedged near the boat's bow. To ensure Dr. Griggs napped as long as possible, his assistant waited to reach the docks before tapping the boss's shoulder. Starting up one dark night, the doctor stepped wide and wrong and tumbled into the water. When he surfaced, he'd lost both his watch and prized Stetson. As legend tells it, back on solid ground, he remarked on neither loss. Worldly possessions only, that hat and watch, when his purpose, his mission, was to save lives, which he proceeded to do that evening, dripping.

*

Also a physician, Anton Pavlovich Chekhov. Also someone born and raised in a water-edged community—in Chekhov's case, a Black Sea coastal town. A medical man, a literary man, a writer already celebrated in St. Petersburg at the age of 26 and already, age 26, made peevish by fame.

From a letter addressed to his uncle: "Every newspaper report about me agitates. My stories are read at public recitations, wherever I go people point at me, I am overwhelmed with acquaintances, and so on, and so on. I have not a day of peace…."

From another letter to the same uncle: "My work is nervous, disturbing and involving strain."

At 27, the young author published "Sleepy," a short story that concludes with an exhausted nurse strangling the fretful baby in her care and collapsing to the floor where she "laughs with delight that she can sleep, and in a minute is sleeping as sound as the dead."

That same year Chekhov overnighted with the Holy Mountain monks. The brothers themselves, he wrote to his sister, were "pleasant" enough, but it wasn't a restful layover. His mattress was "pan-cake like…the services endless. At midnight they ring for matins, at five for early mass…. Before every service one hears in the corridors the…sound of a bell and a monk runs along crying in the voice of a creditor…'Please come to matins!'"

"A Dreary Story," published when the author was 29, is a six-part fiction. The story's narrator, 62-year-old emeritus medical professor Nikolay Stepanovitch, suffers "accursed sleeplessness." If asked "what constituted the chief and fundamental feature of my existence now, I should answer insomnia," declares Chekhov's character. "To lie awake at night means to be at every moment conscious of being abnormal."

Restless, tubercular, grieving for his dead brother, 30-year-old Chekhov departed for Sakhalin Island and its penal colony. Officially his purpose was to take a census of the 10,000 convicts, conduct interviews and file a report. Unofficially the trip had all the earmarks of desperate flight.

Five thousand miles across the Siberian wilderness, three thousand by troika along a dirt *trakt.* Lake Baikal, he crossed by steamer. Another thousand rough-going *versts* to reach the Amur River. Final destination: the North

Pacific.

"Travelling and not sleeping at night, one prizes sleep above everything," he wrote to his publisher.

And posted that letter when?

Soon after entering Siberia, the first leg of a long, long, long, long journey. And sleep, sleep already a fantasy.

*

As did Chekhov's hosts, monks everywhere forfeit sleep to pray—part and parcel of their contract with God. Benedict of Nursia, son of a Roman nobleman, alive and praying in the sixth century, set a high bar for monk behavior with his rules regulating monastic life. Among the highlights:

Enter a monastery, remain till death.

Keep busy.

Remain silent unless spoken to.

Obey the abbot's orders without question.

Be chaste.

Own nothing.

The Benedictines went about their business, spiritual and otherwise, but not all among the order were content. The reformers (the French Cistercians) believed too many Benedictines were failing to live up to St. Benedict's strict guidelines. The Cistercians donned habits of unbleached white (versus Benedictine black), prayed often, slept even less than the Benedictines, and, when neither praying nor sleeping, acquired property. Land grabbers, the Cistercians. Agro-expansionists. Soon they'd accumulated more acres than the core brothers could maintain, even if sleep and prayer were dispensed with altogether. Additional bodies were needed to tend the sheep and work the harvest. For that task, the Cistercians recruited lay brothers from the surrounding villages: young, strong, illiterate fellows whose prayer schedules were more flexible, who could, for instance, sleep in at matins. They needed the rest, those lay brothers. In the fields they worked harder than mules.

Is backbreaking manual labor preferable to sleep deprivation, or sleep deprivation preferable to backbreaking labor?

A ridiculous wonder/query. Who among us truly gets to choose?

*

Mosquitoes, demons of the Diptera order (a.k.a. The True Flies), don't waste nighttime sleeping. They feed. The female of the species happily sucks the blood of monk, atheist, pious saint or wanton sinner. Free of religious prejudice, she doesn't discriminate between the holy and less so. If there's blood to be had, she's interested.

There are 2,500 mosquito species in the world. Two hundred of those species can be found in the United States. To be exposed to/bitten by 77 of the 200 varieties, it's not necessary to leave the state of Florida where a new species was discovered as recently as 2001.

Mosquitoes are capable of flying up to 20 miles from their stagnant water hatching sites. Ponds, pools, bird baths, clogged ditches—any little bit of non-flowing wetness will suffice. In addition to vampires, garlic supposedly repels mosquitoes by interfering with the mosquito's sensory capabilities and therefore with the mosquito's ability to zero in on human prey.

A horror story involving mosquitoes (not vampires).

Time: late evening. Setting: derelict farmhouse in upper New York state. Obstacles between me and the bathroom I needed to get to: 20 or so sleeping bags filled with snoozing climbers and climber attachés. Because the bathroom door didn't fully close, I didn't turn on the light. Eventually, crouching in that dim and fetid space, I noticed that the north wall looked darker than it should, even in night shadow. Add to that disquiet, the darkness jittered. Not from any drug-induced hallucination on my part, from mosquitoes: a larger mass of mosquitoes than I, a Southern swamp girl, had ever seen. Before I could finish up my business, a chunk of that mass recolonized on me.

Conditions and/or beings attractive to mosquitoes:

Tropical climates.

Sweaty bodies.

People who eat bananas. (See Dr. Janet Starr's *Healthy Newsletter*, 2003.)

Carbon dioxide fumes (i.e., anyone who exhales).

Darkness.

People trying to sleep.

A current posting on the BBC website archly confirms the mosquito's "genetic predisposition for flying in one's ear, particularly when one is trying to sleep. Best bet is to give in and ignore them.... Experience has shown that only those with the patience of a monk will succeed at this."

In summary: eat salt (not sugar), breathe in (never out), stay clear of Florida and heat, gorge on garlic (just in case), become a monk, give up on sleep.

Or accept being sucked on.

*

People who can't sleep and also hate mosquitoes?

Cyber gabbers.

"It's not just that mosquitoes are active at night, it's that they are in your room and they hide somewhere, you go looking for them and can't find them, you give up, turn off the light and start going to sleep, but JUST as you are going into that sleepy hazy state, they attack, it happens every time!"

"I used to take melatonin...took it for 150 days straight. Then it stopped working.... I've had dark rings under my eyes for years and years."

"Concentrate on breathing. You know, think 'in out in out' until your mind clears. That helps me."

"Whenever I'm feeling particularly wide awake I watch porn."

"fucked up sleepin patterns are not fun."

"YOU'RE NOT PSYCHOTIC! None of you! A truly psychotic person would be relishing in the surreal effect which sleep deprivation can cause."

Not psychotic.

Not relishing surreal effects.

Just online in the middle of the night, bitching to strangers.

And that counts as improvement precisely how?

*

The year of Chekhov's birth in Taganrog, Charles Dickens, in London, published *The Uncommercial Traveller*, a collection of essays that included "Night Walks."

To introduce the piece, give it context, give it gravitas, Dickens wrote: "Some years ago, a temporary inability to sleep, referable to a distressing impression, caused me to walk about the streets all night."

Referable to a distressing impression in the phraseology of the nineteenth century.

fucked up sleepin patterns in the phraseology of century twenty-one.

Either/or, I take the point.

What I'm not doing while taking the point:

Night-walking the streets of London or Gregory Road.

Logging Siberian *versts* in a troika.

Shoving a boat across the frozen Currituck Sound.

Writing in (or not in) code in a diary.

Praying silently or aloud.

Being bled by mosquitoes.

What I *am* doing is not sleeping. What I am is awake. Helplessly, hopelessly awake, in the bedroom of a house built on a plot of land that slopes, on a street that dead-ends.

In the End

Obits, Life Bits

For 15 years I've been a death reporter, a death summarizer, an editor of death. Part time, freelance contract. No medical benefits.

The pregnant, young and on-the-move obit writer I replaced spent her last Saturday in town training me in the fine art and subtle niceties of obit writing for the university newsletter. And what a wet Saturday it was. A dreary, dismal day on a dreary, dismal campus. Because it was the weekend, parking didn't pose a problem. It would ever after, but that day, no. As arranged, I met her at a Hansel and Gretel-style bungalow, the Home Economics lab turned Alumni House. My predecessor had worked, and for several years more I would continue to work, in a converted bedroom on the second floor. That afternoon, our two chairs wedged side by side in an alcove, she took me through the process. If information went missing from the published news clip, it was my responsibility to call the family and obtain the details.

Panic found a drum in my chest and beat it.

I had assumed that I would be dealing in paper only. Accumulating, parsing, typing up accounts of death. When I said yes to the job, I had no idea I'd be interacting with the bereaved.

Because my predecessor announced she'd be leaving the state as well as the city, I felt safe in assuming she wouldn't be returning to check up on whether or not I followed instructions. I nodded understanding (and implied agreement), rain wriggling on the windowpane. For the record, in 15 years I've called and pumped exactly one new widow for details, my first Monday on the job. It was a horrid, excruciating experience. In an effort to avoid ever repeating that experience, I snooped about to see who else dealt with the alumni clippings. The receptionist stuffed them in my mail slot, but neither she nor anyone higher on the org chart appeared to read or care what those pieces of newsprint did or didn't contain. That discovery left the freelancer free to formulate and enact (on the sly) a new obit policy. No more prying into the specifics of a stranger's death. No more interrupting and intruding on a family's grief. No more distressing and disturbing mourners. Because such practices, you understand, distressed and disturbed *me*. The family of the deceased? Maybe, maybe not.

If the dead's degree and major aren't to be found in the university's database, I've been known to fudge. Ignore the reality that students change majors and graduates change careers and usually a "likely" major suggests itself—business, nursing, physical education. In 15 years, no one has called the office to complain about a misstated major, a record (I rationalize) that vindicates the malfeasance.

But of course it may be grief that keeps the survivors from telephoning.

It may be incapacitating grief.

The obituary notices I vet typically adhere to standard summations. Educational degrees, career achievements and honors, charitable contributions, church and club memberships, military service, hobbies, the year he/she retired to that ranch in the Sierras, the condo in Palm Springs, the assisted living facility in Hayward. A third- or fourth-generation Californian, a citizen of the U.S. since 1908 or 1985. An Army man, a corporate boss, a harpsichordist, a homemaker, a teacher, a cop. A St. Vincent hospital volunteer. A Legos collector. A world traveller. A hockey fan. A 30-year Rotarian. An avid skier. A tenor in a barbershop quartet. Survived by. Died of. Age 98, age 64, age 41.

My father's obituary, laminated and sent "in tribute" by Raleigh, North Carolina's *News and Observer*, is dated February 27, 1985 and contains three brief paragraphs. It doesn't mention my father's occupation (farmer) or hobbies (horseshoes, fishing) or that he won a baseball scholarship to Wake Forest College and gave it up to help his father in the fields while two of his brothers went to war in Europe. It doesn't mention his church affiliation (Providence Baptist) or that he had served the congregation twice as deacon. It doesn't mention that, in the early 1950s, a contingent of Shawboro citizens asked Dubby to become their mayor, an honorific he declined and with that refusal ended the nominating committee's interest in or search for a mayor. Nor does Dubby's obit mention what killed him: a heart attack, at the breakfast table, my mother the single witness. But it does list his survivors: a mother, five siblings, a wife and two children, one in California.

Very early in the morning, Pacific Standard Time, the director of Dorland Mountain Colony came to my lizard-infested writer-in-residence cottage overlooking the then undeveloped town of Temecula with a message to call home. The shack containing the community's one telephone was dark and missing a fourth wall. I could hear the painter in the studio next door making his morning coffee, the faint murmur of his radio. When a voice I didn't recognize answered my parents' telephone in Shawboro, I could only think to identify myself.

"Kathy, hon," Ann Ferebee, friend and neighbor, said. "Your daddy had a heart attack this morning." And I said: "He's in the hospital?" And she said, "No, hon, no." And then, as I recall, I started screaming, and she said: "Get hold of yourself now. Get hold of yourself." And then I said I'd call again as soon as I got to the airport. And then she said: "Okay, hon, okay."

I booked a flight, got to San Diego and the airport, but I couldn't and can't tell you how. Because I was reading Patricia Bosworth's biography of Diane Arbus, I took it with me on the plane but never opened it in transit. I sat next to a young man in a uniform representing which service branch I can't remember. I do remember he sat very still and erect throughout the flight and stayed in his seat during the brief layover when I made my third trip to the lavatory, that trip to puke. I am an uneasy flier because like all uneasy fliers I expect the plane to crash before reaching its destination. A friend of mine said she stopped being afraid to fly when she stopped caring whether she lived or died. On that flight home I shared her indifference. I was in shock, in many ways always will be, about losing my father. If the world didn't contain Dubby, it wasn't a world to covet.

When I deplaned in Norfolk and started toward the terminal lobby, I could see my brother, beyond the glass, pacing back and forth. He wasn't looking in my direction, in any direction. I told myself on that walk that I had to "get hold of myself" because my brother was so distraught. If I collapsed, he would immediately put aside his own grief to tend to mine and I couldn't let him do that. Both of us had lost a father. Both.

It was after midnight when we got out of the car in Shawboro, met first by the dogs and then by my mother in the dark yard. In the house, cousins, uncles, aunts—a space dense with people, overloaded with food. Because my mother couldn't bear to sleep in the room she had slept in with my father, she lay on the couch and I on the floor beside her, holding her hand, neither of us sleeping. Throughout the night she kept describing how Dubby died, his chair falling backward, her attempts to resuscitate, reliving that failure again and again. He had chopped more than a cord of wood the day before. He had coughed throughout the previous night. He, they, assumed the pain in his chest was indigestion, something an antacid could reduce, relieve, overcome.

Cause of death: ischemic heart disease. Time of death: 8:50 a.m., February 26. Age of deceased: 67. DOA, Albemarle Hospital. No autopsy performed.

Day and night people came. People I should have recognized but didn't.

People from high school, from grammar school, third and fourth cousins from Weeksville, one of whom exclaimed in wonder about me: "Why, she looks just like her Aunt Madeline!"

From behind me, my brother said: "You do *not* look like Madeline!"

Trying to console his sister in matters in which she might still be consoled.

The funeral director's son came with a paper bag containing the clothes and accessories my father had been wearing when a hospital doctor pronounced him DOA: green work pants and shirt, a watch with a sprung wristband, suede work shoes. No socks. Dubby often came to breakfast sockless, in unlaced shoes. When the emissary handed over that bundle, I courteously, absurdly, thanked him. Then I set the bag on the roots of a pine tree, returned to the living room and signaled my brother from the doorway. Together we burned our father's effects in an oil drum behind the shed while simultaneously, ten miles away, it might be argued, some mortician's assistant was burning the body of our father.

Dubby's funeral service counted as the first casket-less, body-less service the Providence Baptist minister had conducted, he told us. He did not seem to approve of the precedent. After we returned home, a relation by marriage, let's call her Thelma, settled her ample flesh in my father's favorite chair. A newcomer to the family, she was my father's eldest brother's second wife, and she was one of those Southern women who injure, and who mean to injure, under the guise of sympathy. With no preamble, Thelma asked my mother where and when she planned to move. "What do you mean, Thelma? This is my home," my mother answered in a voice too tentative, too faint, too fragile. Thelma didn't care. Thelma wasn't listening. Thelma was stirring the pot, enlarging on the perils of widowhood, expressing "concern" about my mother living in a house all alone, way back on a dirt road, no one close enough to hear her scream if she screamed—and much more in that vein. Because it would have further upset my mother, I didn't tell Thelma to shut the fuck up, shove her ass out the door or bitch-slap her cheeks until they flamed as red as mine. But the forced restraint made me vibrate on the couch while my mother leaned back in her chair and closed her eyes and Thelma chattered on and on.

Within a week of Dubby's death, his mother, my grandmother, Dora died. She was 95. The last year of her discontented life she spent more discontent in a miserable nursing home, hoping hourly to die. Dora's remains were not cremated. Drained, embalmed, rouged and stored in a casket, her corpse awaited in-ground burial. To plan Dora's funeral, her children and the grandchild who represented Dubby gathered at Aunt Vivian's house. No dissension, minimal discussion, as per usual with the Meadses. Aunt Vivian suggested a bier arrangement of pink carnations and baby's breath. The women present said, in essence: "Whatever you think, Vivian." The men looked at their laps and nodded.

A rainy, windy day, the day of Dora's funeral, the second in 10 days for the Meads clan. At the gravesite, the pallbearers stood in mud, one of them my brother. When I hugged Aunt Vivian and commiserated with her loss, she said: "No, hon, no. It was for the best." For the best or otherwise, they were both gone: Dora and Dubby.

As often happens with survivors, in the wake of my father's death, I dreamed him alive. In the early dreams, he did normal Dubby stuff: worked on the combine, played with the dog, cleaned out his tackle box, bent down to pinch a clod of field dirt. But even within the context of normality, I, the dreamer, sensed something off, some indefinable something not quite right. In the next phase of sleep grieving, I dreamed Dubby had deserted us, run off, lit out for elsewhere, disappeared without cause or explanation. I cried hard during that dream and cried harder when I woke from it. Eventually I dreamed of telling, of having to tell, Dubby he was dead, of being the bearer of that awful, awful news and watching him sorrowfully accept the verdict that he no longer existed, both of us grieving together. At the end of those dreams he simply faded away, head down, shoulders slumped, resigned to his fate and I incapable in dream or in life of countermanding that cosmic order.

I forfeited the remainder of my Dorland residency to finish out the month with my mother, help her write thank-you notes, make sure she ate. My brother joined us on the weekends. On one of those weekends, he and I took the boat and Dubby's ashes out on Indiantown Creek. My mother didn't accompany us. When we reached one of Dubby's favorite fishing holes, my brother cut the motor and, trying to spare me, as always, told me to look away. For his sake, I turned my head. I didn't trust that the ashes in the box were Dubby's ashes. But even if I had believed we were dumping matter that had been our father into Indiantown Creek, the process wouldn't have concluded my grieving. It wouldn't have served as my final goodbye.

During the month I stayed with my mother, two other Shawborians died, one elderly of natural causes, the other middle-aged and by his own hand. Suicides and gruesome accidental deaths aren't rarities in Shawboro. Before blinking lights and electrical crossbars were installed beside the main set of railroad tracks, several carloads of teenagers came to a bad end, racing night trains. A classmate of my brother's came home from school to find her mother hanging in the hallway. Got off the bus, opened the door and saw between ribbons of afternoon sunlight her mother's dangling corpse. A classmate of mine, a logger, was decapitated when a cable snapped. Only 36, the father of two young children. Death resonates in a small community. Even if you don't intimately know the dead, chances are you know well one or another of his or her kin. My mother, my brother and I all knew the middle-aged fellow newly dead. A farmer, he'd struggled to support a family on the profits of a small farm. Recently he'd become convinced his cancer had returned, despite the dissenting opinion of his doctor. In the middle of a weekday afternoon, he drove his pickup to the edge of one of his fields, walked a half mile into the woods, and turned his hunting rifle on himself. Ann Ferebee called with the news. When I answered the phone and she said "Kathy, hon," my heart seized up all over again.

Eventually I had to leave my mother's house and my mother alone in her widowhood, a wife who'd expected to die before her husband, a daughter who hadn't expected to live past 54, the age her mother, Luna, had died. After Dubby's funeral, my mother composed her own obituary. I have seen it because she has shown it to me, as well as where she keeps it. So I'll know—in the event. She wrote it in blue pen on a half sheet of lined notebook paper. There are phrases scratched out and written over, but even so it runs shorter than Dubby's published obituary. In content, it's personally modest. She expends most of her word count on family ties. She names her parents, her husband, her children and her membership in Providence Baptist. In the final sentence she announces the funeral home in which the visitation will take place and leaves a blank for the date to be filled in.

Reading my mother's obituary standing beside her creeped me out, but my reaction in the moment wasn't of primary concern. My mother wanted assurances that I knew exactly where to find it. That I would remember. That "in the confusion," I'd still not forget. That I would go directly to the drawer beside the table beside the rocker and retrieve it the instant I returned from my state of residence ever so far away. And those assurances I gave.

My father has been dead more than 20 years. My mother lives on. She has attended scores of funerals since Dubby died; she and I have attended a dozen or more together. Cremation is no longer the novelty it once was, even in Shawboro. My cousin Dot's husband, Ken, requested cremation and got his wish. Even if I'd missed the funeral proper, I would have paid Dot a condolence call because Dot, in an act of pure kindness, hired my newly widowed mother to work part time in her Elizabeth City dress shop. Dot didn't need the help—business was slow—but the job gave my mother a reason to leave the house and netted her a paycheck while she stitched two quilts. So my mother and I both had a soft spot for Dot, if not for Ken.

Ken's service was held on Bells Island. He'd been a recreational sailor and wanted his ashes scattered in Currituck Sound. Since my mother (who can't swim) wanted to be part of the water entourage, I got her into the tippy boat with the help of cousin Stanley, Dot's brother. In a kind of funeral flotilla, various skiffs headed out into the chop, each passenger holding a white carnation. Midway to our goal, my mother let go of my arm and her carnation to clutch her head and moan: "This *swaying*!" If she stood up, lost her balance and pitched headfirst into the water, I sincerely hoped she'd take cousin Stanley with her because I was nursing a grudge against cousin Stanley who'd greeted me with the slur: "You're pale as death yourself, girl. Next time get some sun before coming home."

Dot, her two sons and their wives occupied the lead boat. The fleet was to form a circle; Ken's ashes were to be scattered; we were then to toss flowers in the general direction of the last of him. Such was the plan. It fell to Ken and Dot's younger son, beer bottle in one hand, ash can in the other, to perform the final honors. Those ten digits engaged, he had none to spare for a wind test, which meant he didn't correct for direction, velocity or updraft, which meant that much of what he dumped, whatever it was he dumped, landed on the dead's immediate family whose choices were to ignore that coating or to treat Ken's remnants the way they treated lint.

"Jesus Christ!" cousin Stanley blurted.

My mother claimed to believe he'd uttered that cry in prayer.

The botched water ceremony, however, set her brooding about bodies buried in-ground. Heading back toward Meads Road, she insisted we stop by the Sears family graveyard, located off Tull's Creek Road in the field behind the house she had grown up in. Not the best of ideas, I thought in advance of the detour, but she was adamant. Every year she donates some undisclosed (to me) amount of money to her dead sister Pearl's "boys," aged 60 and older, to caretake the site: mow the grass, repair the fence as necessary, dust off the headstones. I feared our stop-by was, at its core, a visit to check up on the caretakers rather than the dead, and so it was. We beat our way through brown soybeans to the graves of her parents, two brothers, Pearl, Pearl's stillborn child and assorted others. Outraged by the thriving weeds and the disrespect that neglect (in her mind) confirmed, she pursed hard her lips. "Soon as we get home, I'm calling Bill."

"I'd wait until tomorrow," I said.

"*Soon as we get home*," she repeated.

I suggested the stall for several reasons. When we left Dot's, Bill was sprawled on a lawn chair, drunk but still drinking. Even if he'd since been driven home by his abstemious wife, he'd be in no shape to parry his aunt's accusations.

Wasted breath on my part. My mother was riled. Into the house she whipped, snatched up the telephone, dialed and laid hard into the poor sop who answered.

Now in failing health, my mother laments that neither of her children lives closer: in the county, in the community, next door. At least once during every telephone conversation, she asks when I'm coming home. I return as often as I can. Ditto my brother. We have not deserted her, but we have not stayed nearby—at this juncture, an equally unforgivable choice.

When we are with her, to take her mind off how soon our visits will end, my brother and I have both become expert diversionists. We spend a significant part of our time in the car, driving around, an activity distracting for her and entertaining for us. We pass a house, she catches us up on the latest news of the residents within. We pass a field, she tells us who sold those acres to whom and the business rumored to be going "in" where corn has been.

The last time she and I drove past the Culbertsons' house, she noticed Elaine's minivan in the driveway.

"She must be in there clearing out her mother's things," my mother reasoned. "Let's stop in a minute—just to speak."

We parked behind the minivan. We knocked at the door of the closed-in breezeway. Elaine duly appeared.

"Come in, come in," she said. No, no, she said. Glad for the interruption. Delighted to sit and talk a spell.

The last time I'd been in the house, Elaine and I sat at the kitchen table, sorting photos for the high school yearbook. I asked if I could take a look around and she waved me on. "If you can get through the piles."

A small house I'd remembered as spacious. Lamps, dishes, glassware, pots, pans, a rusty birdcage. A bowling ball and bag. (Margaret, Elaine's mother, had been a league bowler and a good one.) Portable appliances, pillows, sheets, magazines, stools high and low, board games, placemats, knickknacks whole and chipped. Toiletries, ashtrays, power tools, bath towels, dishtowels, canned food. Wire. String. Rubber bands. The walls were bare, the floors layered, heap upon heap.

"Kathy and Craig are going to have the same mess when I go," my mother was saying when I rejoined them on the breezeway. Flippant—her public pose.

Back in the car, just the two of us, she said: "Don't just throw out my dress suits. Some of them are barely worn. When we get home, I'll show you which ones I mean. They're the ones hanging in the closet in your brother's room. Remember that. Not the closet in my room. The back bedroom. Will you remember or do I need to leave a note?"

Because Dora's death so quickly followed Dubby's, I didn't have chance to properly—or singularly—mourn my grandmother. Dora's absence got mingled in with the other. It didn't, couldn't, overshadow the loss of Dubby. If there is an afterlife and Dora made it there, I doubt she'd give a possum's ass in what manner or to what extent one grandchild of 12 mourned or didn't mourn her passing. Dora didn't like "weeping and wailing" for any reason, death included. She expected her blood kin to be tough, physically and emotionally. She despised sentimentality and those who trucked in it. She had less use for "overwrought" than she had for weakness (as defined by Dora). Her marriage had not been happy in her estimation and, as a widow, she let everyone know—often—how much she loathed and had loathed husband Jack. To avoid being buried beside him in Weeksville, she bought a single plot for herself in a cemetery in Moyock, two counties east.

When Dora purchased her gravesite, the location probably appeared more idyllic than it has since become. Wedged between a savings and loan bank and a car dealership, Dora's eternal resting spot is now a drop zone for pollutants generated by a four-lane, beach-access highway. To get to the Norfolk, Virginia, airport from Shawboro, it's necessary to drive through Moyock and by Dora's cemetery. Regardless, I hadn't entered that cemetery since Dora's funeral. Part of my reluctance was job-related, an occupational hazard. After years of summing up lives in abbreviated obituary form, I wasn't keen to see Dora's 95 years reduced to tombstone script.

The afternoon I finally did steer car and self through the entrance gates, I could feel the resistance rebuilding. But I was *there* and, very aware of my dead grandmother's contempt for the lily-livered, stopped the car, got out and started traipsing about.

Eventually I found and recognized her row. Squinting, fully prepared to scowl or flinch, I approached Dora's rectangle of grass. Close enough to read the inscription on her granite marker, I blinked and superstitiously glanced behind me. Then I reread what I hadn't misread the first time. Then I started cackling—loud enough to challenge the roar of traffic and send skittish crows flying. Because in a cemetery of loving mother and wife tributes, Dora's gravestone is etched "loving mother" and not a syllable more. At the family meeting at Aunt Vivian's house, gravestone inscriptions were not discussed. Who, then, had served as Dora's editor? A Meads who believed in hauntings, I'd guess.

If I believed in the practice of burying bones, if I wanted my own bones buried and marked, I'd want the lines above my skull cribbed from Stephen Dunn's poem "California, This is Minnesota Speaking."

I am so in control/ my dream is/ to be slightly out of control.

Except that would be too many words for granite, for a gravestone.

Perhaps, instead, six words from the poet brother of Diane Arbus.

While life is, life is long.

Like night.

Acknowledgments

Essays in this collection first appeared whole, in part, in altered form, and occasionally under different titles in the following print and online journals:

Agni Online: "On Reading and Rereading *The Mind of the South* in No Place Southern"
American Letters and Commentary: "Beds, a Reverie"*
Blood Lotus: "Work, for the Day is Coming—Louise Bourgeois's *Insomnia Drawings*
Chautauqua Literary Journal: "Counterproductive Bedtime Stories"*
Chicago Quarterly Review: "Among the Wakeful, These"
Crab Orchard Review, American South Special Issue: "Neighbor Trim, Also Awake"*
Crazyhorse: "What Lies in Closets"
Drunken Boat: "Ruth Paine's 2 a.m. Letter"**
Fugue: "The Making of an Insomniac"
Natural Bridge: "Salton Sea, Dreamscape"
Pilgrimage: "Craters in the Sand (Why No One Should Sleep Easy)"
Prick of the Spindle: "Four Days & Four White Nights"
Southern Humanities Review: "Undone: Bessie Wallis of Baltimore"
The Southern Review: "The Rise and Fall of Sheriff Glenn Brinkley"
storySouth: Portions of "Obits, Life Bits"
Superstition Review: "Relativism: the Size of the Tsar in Vegas"
Vibrant Gray: "Asleep but Not Abed"; reprinted in *South Loop Review*

*Notable essays, *The Best American Essays* series (Houghton Mifflin Harcourt), Robert Atwan, Series Editor:

- "Beds, a Reverie" (2009)
- "Counterproductive Bedtime Stories" (2010)
- "Neighbor Trim, Also Awake" (2012)

**Editors' Choice Award in Nonfiction, Panliterary Competition, *Drunken Boat*: "Ruth Paine's 2 a.m. Letter" (titled "On Fighting the Temptation to Fictionalize Marina Oswald")

About the Author

Kat Meads is the author of the essay collection *Born Southern and Restless* and other books of prose and poetry. She has received nonfiction awards from *New Letters, Lyra* and *Drunken Boat* and Notable Essays recognition in the *Best American Essays* series. A native of North Carolina, she lives in California and teaches in Oklahoma City University's Red Earth MFA program.

www.ingramcontent.com/pod-product-compliance
Lightning Source LLC
Chambersburg PA
CBHW020523120726
47904CB00003B/947

* 9 7 8 1 6 2 2 8 8 0 3 9 3 *